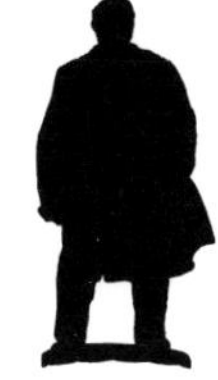

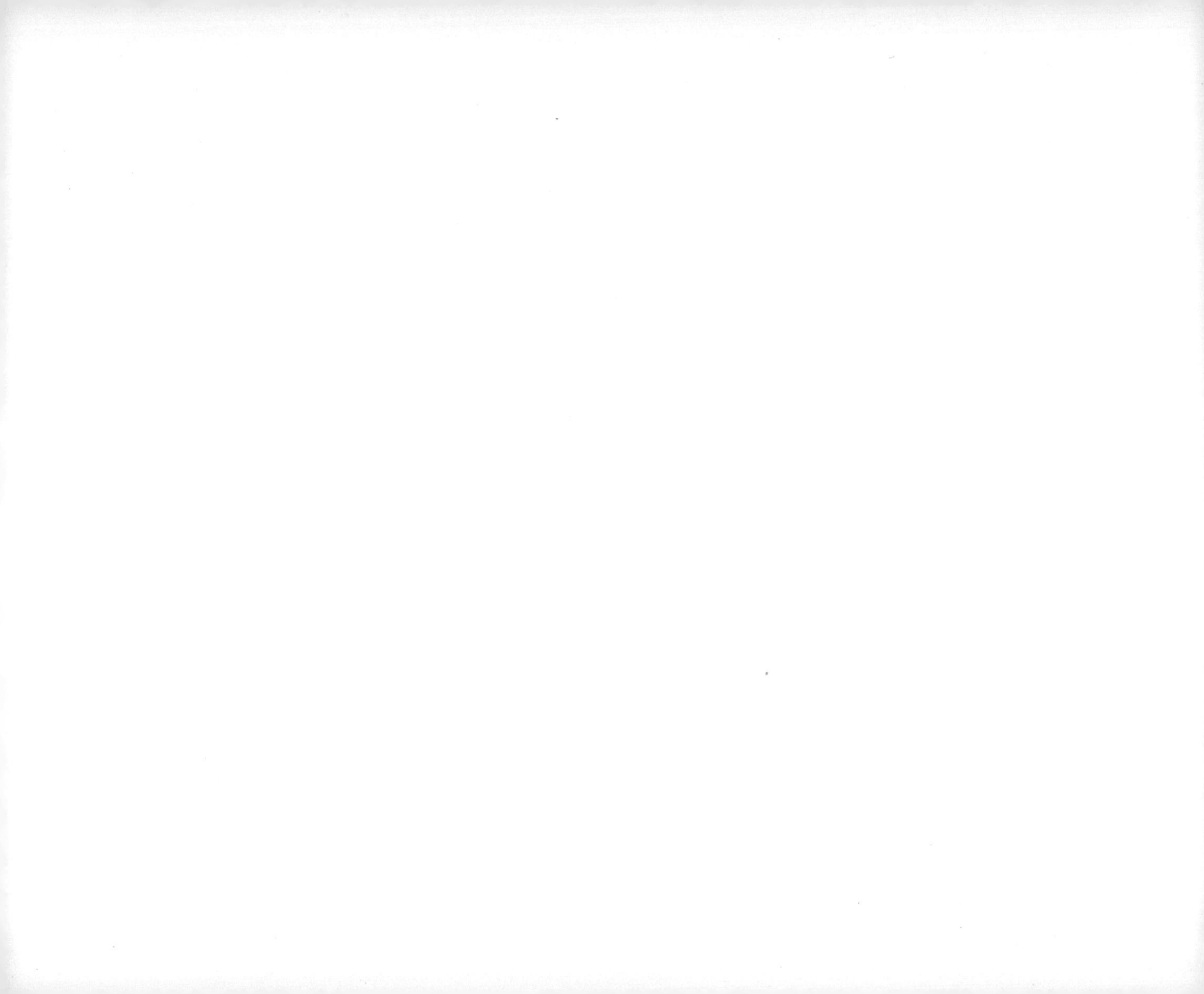

LOOK ING FOR LENIN

NIELS ACKERMANN
SÉBASTIEN GOBERT

FUEL

LENIN AFTER THE FALL

MYROSLAVA HARTMOND

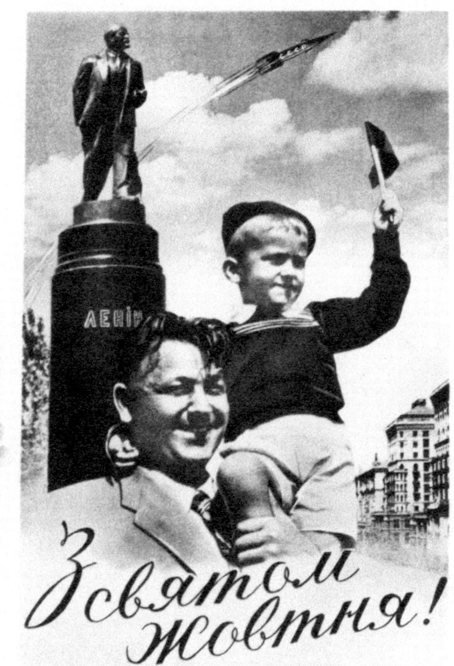

Happy October!
Photomontage of rocket and the
Bessarabska Lenin statue on
Taras Shevchenko Boulevard.
Sculptor: S. Merkurov
Kyiv
Postcard, 1959
(pp.171-173)

Monuments as propaganda were a unifying feature of the public landscape throughout the fifteen Soviet republics and the satellite states. Statues, busts, arches, obelisks, cenotaphs, victory columns, memorial plaques, eternal flames, decorative detailing and mosaics... the collective space was permeated with Communist symbolism and aesthetics. Of these, the serial form of Vladimir Lenin was undoubtedly the most prominent.

Following the break-up of the Soviet Union in December 1991, each newly independent state dealt with this physical legacy differently. Ukraine's Leninfall – the toppling of monuments to the Communist figurehead by activists in the months after the 2013–14 Euromaidan protests in favour of closer European integration and an end to the corrupt pro-Kremlin regime – presents a particularly interesting case. The practice of erecting statues to reinforce subjugation is nothing new, and their toppling is a hallmark of regime overhaul and popular revolution. Yet in the context of the Ukrainian Euromaidan or Revolution of Dignity – which resulted in the ousting of President Viktor Yanukovych and the reinstatement of the 2004 constitutional amendments – the anachronistic Lenin statues acquired an unexpected political relevance. Leninfall was a wave of symbolic violence that swept across Ukraine. It exposed tensions within an atomised Ukrainian society and demanded a reassessment of the country's politics of memory.

When Ukraine seceded from the Soviet Union in 1991, it contained an abundance of propaganda in monument form. Although the

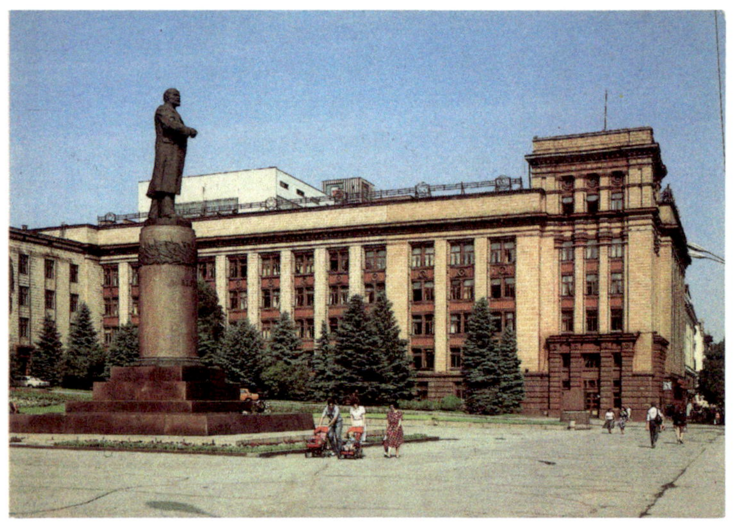

Monument to V. I. Lenin
Sculptors: O. Oliynik,
M. Vronsky
Architect: O. Sidorenko
Dnipropetrovsk
(now Dnipro)
Postcard, 1977
(p.53)

country's Lenin memorials differed in size, composition, material and quality of craftsmanship, they all served the same ideological function. With 5500 individual Lenin statues – compared to 7000 in Russia, 600 in Belarus, 500 in Kazakhstan and a mere 300 in the entire Trans-Caucasus and Central Asian region – the density of monuments per square kilometre was higher in Ukraine than anywhere else in the former USSR. Sculptures of Bolshevik leaders had begun to disappear from the streets of Ukrainian cities in 1990, before the dissolution of the Soviet Union. In a 2013 television interview, Ukrainian writer Yurii Andrukhovych famously remarked on the regional differences in the treatment of Lenin monuments in pre-Euromaidan Ukraine:

garlanded *lieux de mémoire* in the Eastern regions; unnoticed and unkempt relics in the Centre; and virtually non-existent in the West of the country. The Galicia administration in Western Ukraine was the first to authorise the removal of statues of Lenin and Felix Dzerzhinsky, soon followed by other towns in the region.

Another wave of toppling took place after the Orange Revolution of 2004 under President Viktor Yushchenko, who passed a series of memory laws relating to the Holodomor, a Kremlin-engineered Ukrainian famine which claimed the lives of 7 million people in 1932–33. A decree authorised the removal of more than 400 memorials to Communist leaders and the renaming of 3000 locations dedicated

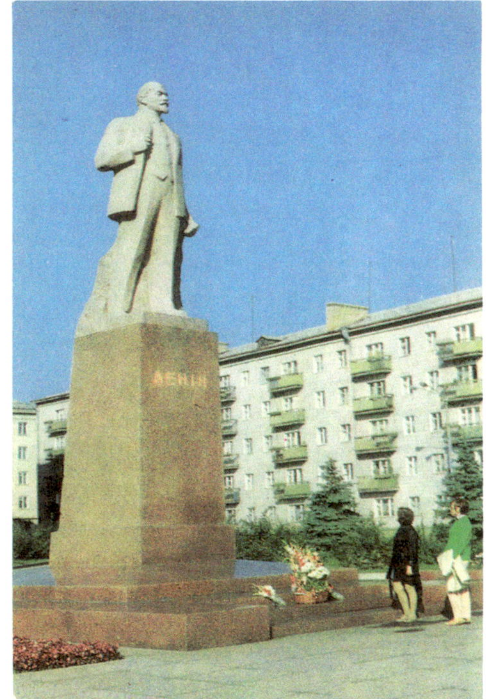

Monument to V. I. Lenin
Sculptors: M. Vronsky, A. Oleinik
Architect: F. Grinchenko
Zhytomyr
Postcard, 1972
(p.51)

to Soviet heroes. Many monuments were destroyed, while others disappeared, resurfacing later in private collections at home and abroad.

Some memorials met more unusual fates. Thirty-two sculptures depicting Lenin, Karl Marx, Friedrich Engels, Dzerzhinsky and Nadezhda Krupskaya (Lenin's wife), alongside a number of literary figures from the Soviet period, were collected from the cities of Simferopol, Odessa, Kyiv and Kherson to be transported to Cape Tarkhankut on the Crimean coast, where they were sunk offshore to create an underwater hall of infamy 15 metres below the surface. Others migrated to an impromptu open-air museum in a former *kolkhoz* (collective farm), the quirky retirement project of a local farmer. Unlike Hungary's Memento Park or Lithuania's Grūtas Park, no

state provision had been made for the collective display of these relics. The majority of monuments remained in situ – and may have continued to occupy their plinths had it not been for the Euromaidan protests and their aftermath.

The protests began as a peaceful demonstration against the pro-Kremlin kleptocracy of the Yanukovych regime. On 8 December 2013, as tensions between protesters and riot police escalated, a group of demonstrators aligned with the far-right Svoboda ('Freedom') Party pulled down the Lenin statue in Taras Shevchenko Boulevard in Kyiv [also known as the Bessarabska Lenin], attacking the monument with cudgels and sledgehammers. This event, widely televised across the globe, was depicted as emblematic by both Russian and Western media. It simultaneously showed two opposing

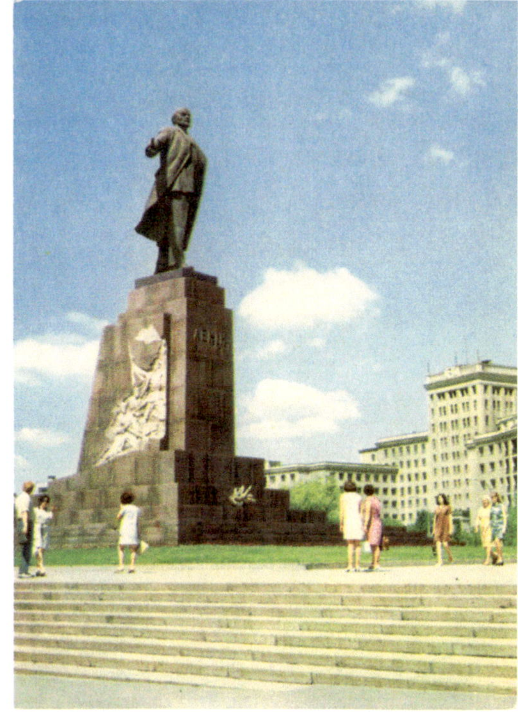

Monument to V. I. Lenin
Sculptors: O. Oliynik, M. Vronsky
Architect: O. Sidorenko
Kharkiv
Postcard, 1974
(p.109)

images of Ukraine: in one, the country was in the grip of a fascist coup; in the other, Ukrainians sought a break with the Soviet past and demonstrated a willingness to embrace Europe. The incident would precipitate 'Leninopad' or Leninfall, a process that reached its climax in February 2014, when 376 Lenins fell in a single month.

Once again, the actions of nationalist groups in the Eastern regions and Crimea were used by Russian media to reinforce the notion that Ukraine had been overrun by far-right extremists who were terrorising local populations. Contemporary artist and writer Yevgenia Belorusets was deeply concerned by the damaging effect extremist voices were having on the world's perception of Ukraine. Her project *Let's Put Lenin's Head Back Together Again!* sought to highlight the issue at a time when there was no public debate on the matter. Interviewed in 2016, she recalled the distress of local citizens when they witnessed activists in balaclavas shouting and saluting as they tore Lenin down. She condemned the conservatism of local administrations, who were afraid to provide information on the whereabouts of the statues since no instructions had been issued by the central authorities. This behaviour exposed the legacy of terror that still permeates Ukrainian regional politics. Moreover, she sought to demonstrate how the political message of the Euromaidan protests had been hijacked by radical groups. Chanting slogans such as 'Freedom or death' and 'Death to our enemies', members brandished the insignia of nationalist groups that had collaborated with the Nazis during

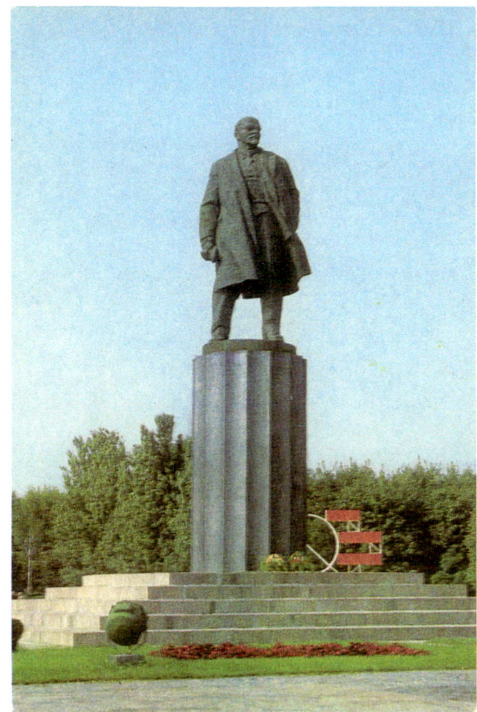

Monument to V. I. Lenin
Sculptor: E. Kuntsevich
Architects: A. Ignashchenko, V. Popov
Kremenchuk
Postcard, 1970
(p.21)

WWII and displayed a portrait of controversial nationalist Stepan Bandera near the central stage. These factions did not represent the political sentiments of the peaceful civil majority — and smashing the Lenin statue was the apogee of their marginal actions.

The forceful purging of the Communist figurehead's images in both urban and rural environments carried deeply revisionist sentiments. During the Soviet period, minor forms of architecture and decorative arts such as mosaics and stained glass may have evaded state control and expressed locally derived themes, but the plinth remained under strict supervision until the last years of Perestroika. The first monument to Lenin in Ukraine was erected in St Sophia Square in Kyiv in the spring of 1919, shortly after the Red Army captured the city. The alabaster statue didn't last long: it was demolished on 31 August 1919 as the Ukrainian People's Republic (UNR) Army and the Volunteer Army entered Kyiv. When the Bolsheviks recaptured the capital in November 1921, Lenin monuments replaced the statuary of the tsarist regime and was established as a prominent feature in all major cities: Kyiv, Dnipropetrovsk (now Dnipro), Chernihiv, Sumy, Kharkiv, Luhansk. Town and village administrations scrambled to erect statues of the Communist leader in an attempt to prove their loyalty to the increasingly repressive regime. These were often made in haste from cheap materials, to be replaced by more permanent versions later.

The Lenin on Taras Shevchenko Boulevard, however, was far from inferior, and aesthetic arguments could certainly have been

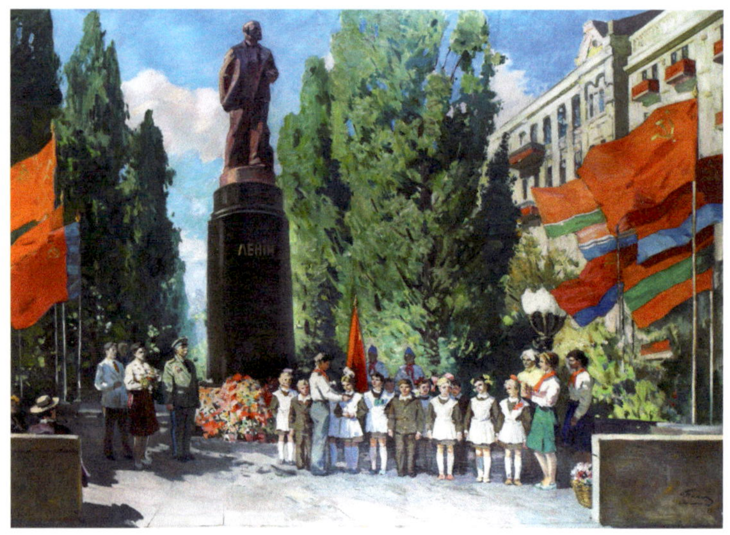

Little Octobrists at the Monument to Vladimir Lenin (1976), Anatoly Plamenitsky. Oil painting depicting the Lenin statue on Taras Shevchenko Boulevard. (pp.171-173)

made for its preservation. A rare example of Soviet monumental sculpture by Sergei Merkurov, the statue was fashioned from red quartzite – a scarce and expensive stone, famously used for the shrine of the Red Chapel of Hapsetshut in Egypt, Napoleon's tomb in Les Invalides in Paris and Lenin's Mausoleum in Moscow's Red Square, an unsettling structure that has been compared to an Aztec teocalli, a Babylonian ziggurat and an Egyptian pyramid. A feature of Kyiv's urban landscape for many decades, the Lenin statue was presented to the city by Stalin in 1946 after its return from the 1939 New York World's Fair. In a 1976 painting by Anatoly Plamenitsky, Merkurov's Lenin, flanked by unfurled flags, presides over a group of Little

Octobrists. The seven-year-olds are admitted into the organisation once the ritual pinning of Lenin's childhood image on to their chests is complete. The central positioning and elongated proportions of the monument are emphatic, aesthetically and ideologically. Like the sacred stones of prehistoric peoples that fascinated Romanian historian of religion Mircea Eliade, Lenin is the focal point of worship on to which the community projects its fantasies of collective endurance.

Of course, the paradox of Leninfall is the temporal disconnect between the end of Communism and the destruction of the statues. There is a noticeable gap between the historic personage of Vladimir Lenin, the personality cult engineered by his successors and the

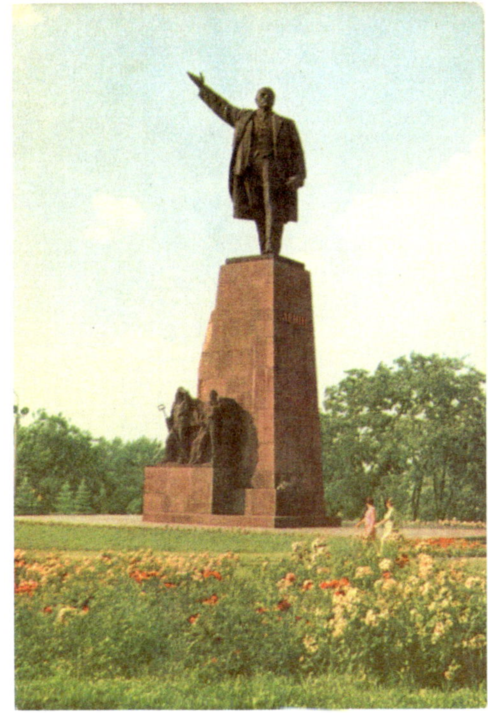

Monument to V. I. Lenin
Zaporizhia
Postcard, 1969
(p.67)

material legacy of that cult. To some, Lenin is an embodiment of evil and destruction, his image the face of an enemy from without, a coloniser, an *other*. Leninfall is catharsis — a collective, ecstatic, performative action that seeks to rewrite Ukraine's national narrative, free from the mistakes of history. The official decommunisation process did not begin until April 2015, and the decommunisation laws passed in May that year effectively exonerated the actions of the activists by turning them into state policy. The law 'On condemning the Communist and National-Socialist totalitarian regimes and prohibiting the use of their symbols' made provision for the removal of the remaining monuments and symbols 'that glorify functionaries of [the] Soviet totalitarian regime', as well as for a thorough overhaul of place names. This and related laws were criticised in an open letter from an international group of 60 experts who voiced a particular concern with the banning of the Communist Party, as well as with the lack of a clear strategy for the facilitation of public debate on memory.

Leninfall is not just an act of violence against history. The empty plinths that litter the towns and villages of Ukraine today, much like the stumps of felled trees, attest to its destructiveness. They become points of convergence for contending visions of national representation, posing the question: What next? 'History hates empty pedestals,' says photographer Donald Weber. His ongoing work exposes the ugliness of the 'decommunised' landscape. Scrawled with slogans or damaged beyond repair, these empty

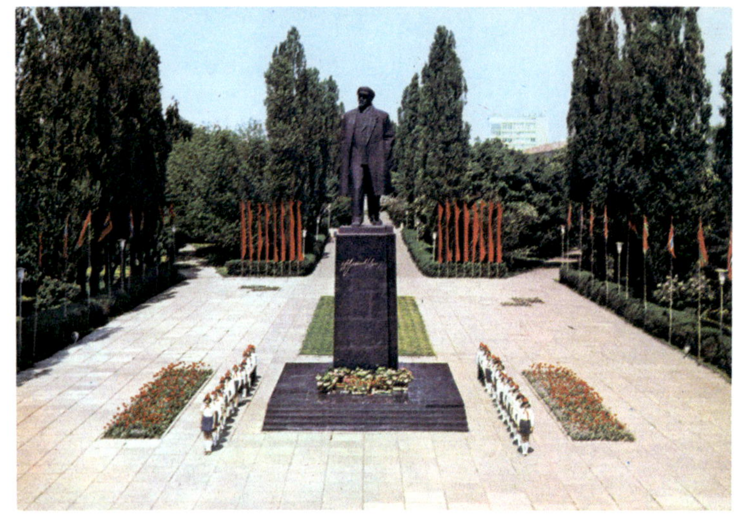

Monument to V. I. Lenin
Chernihiv
Postcard, 1980
(p.107)

plinths in little-known places accentuate the drabness of their surroundings. No longer 'colonised' by Lenin, they nonetheless show little sign of development.

Zhanna Kadyrova's *Monument to a New Monument* (2009) stands in a prosaic village square against a backdrop of chain-link fencing, wooden benches and slate roofs. The veiled figure, made of concrete and broken tiles, is at once incongruously elegant and intrusively officious. It is inherently ironic – statues are usually covered before their unveiling ceremony, but this is more suggestive of a body shrouded for interment. The veil will never be lifted: the plinth is not a battleground, but a burial ground. In the exhibition *Above the Pedestal the Air Condenses in a Dark Cloud*, which premiered at the Škuc Gallery in Ljubljana, Slovenia, in September 2016, the artist Nikita Kadan references the stylite 'pillar dwellers' of the Byzantine era by placing images of lonely ascetics on top of the empty plinths of Soviet monuments still inscribed with the names of the leaders they once commemorated. His figures recall the 14th-century frescoes of Theophanes the Greek at the Church of the Transfiguration of Our Saviour in Novgorod. Kadan and Kadyrova came to prominence as members of Revolutionary Experimental Space (R.E.P.), a group of artists founded after the Orange Revolution in 2004. R.E.P.'s work began with a series of actions

Monument to V. I. Lenin (1946)
Sculptors: M. Vronsky, O. Oliynik, S. Knizhnikov
Architect: M. Makhonko
Sumy
Postcard, 1985
(p.83)

and performances called *Interventions*, which were developed 'in reaction to the politicised public space of the "post-orange" Ukraine' and sought to reconcile the dynamic changes within Ukrainian civil society with the relative stasis of its institutions and infrastructure.

For performance artist Alevtina Kakhidze, the haunting sight of the empty plinth opens up a space for humour. In the early days of Leninfall she cheekily proposed the replacement of all the stone monuments with glass replicas, 'so that no one could say that we don't remember our past here in Ukraine'. Alternatively, she suggested giving every Lenin statue a serial number, reducing them to the status of enlisted soldiers, convicts, or items in a catalogue. Kakhidze insists that humour and irony are the best tools to expose the phantoms that have such agency in the politics and society of post-Soviet Ukraine. In 2015, Oleksandr Milov made international headlines by transforming a rusting Lenin standing in the grounds of an Odessan factory into a monument to *Star Wars* villain Darth Vader. This poignant subversion fits well with the technology-savvy, progressive image the port city strives to present to the world. There are other less skilful, but similarly inspired, examples of Communist monuments that have been 'repurposed' as Cossacks, *hetmans* (military commanders) and superheroes.

Today, not a single Lenin statue remains standing in Ukraine. There has been no consistency in their handling: they have been variously toppled and left unclaimed; stored away by the authorities; broken up or tampered with beyond recognition; or repossessed by hopeful locals. For photographer Niels Ackermann and journalist

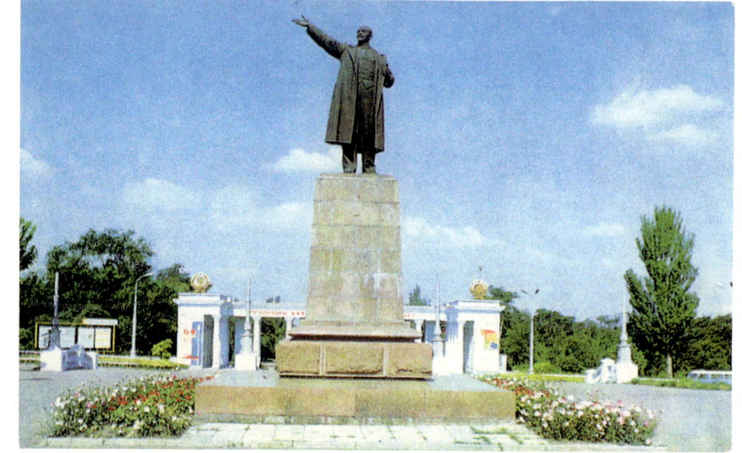

Sébastien Gobert, *Looking for Lenin* is no straightforward cataloguing task. It is an investigation, an obsessional exercise in reconstitution reminiscent of the documentary work produced by the Düsseldorf School of Photography, piecing together a portrait of Ukraine today. The photographs are stark and current, at once deadpan and humorous. In this *catalogue raisonné*, this taxonomy of fallen idols, the mysterious 'White Angel' at the heart of Ackermann's 2016 project of the same name transforms into Lenin, a Lenin after the fall. Here Lenin lies face down in an overgrown field. There he hides in a cupboard under the stairs of a municipal building, or stands awkwardly amid rubble in a private warehouse, a backdrop of Socialist Realist canvases decaying behind him. He shelters under a fruit machine, a relic from a bygone age. He is decapitated and daubed with paint, in the blue-and-yellow colours of the Ukrainian flag. In another photograph, a number of Lenin busts stare from the open boot of a maroon hatchback. And here, nothing remains of him but a dismembered Gogolian nose.

Ackermann and Gobert's Arthurian quest for the holy grail of all Lenins – the very same Bessarabska Ilyich that was the first Lenin to fall – continues to this day. It is rumoured to be in the possession of a wealthy collector of military memorabilia. Its head recently surfaced during a protest by the Svoboda Party, only to disappear again. The empty plinth where it once stood, all 7 metres of it, has

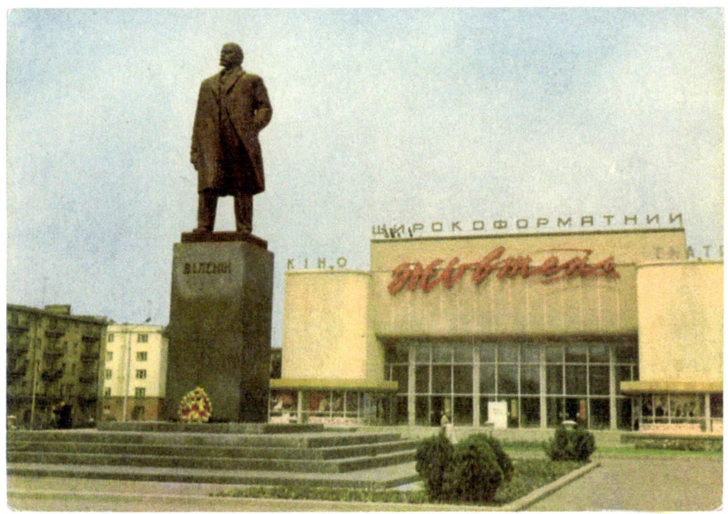

Monument to V. I. Lenin
Sculptor: M. Bronsky
Rivne
Postcard, 1970
(p.97)

become the location for the IZOLYATSIA Art Fund's *Social Contract* an art intervention project similar to that of the Fourth Plinth on London's Trafalgar Square – which brings temporary installations to what would be an otherwise desolate spot. No design has yet been agreed upon as a permanent replacement.

Once again, Ukraine is at a cross-roads, choosing between the Western tendency towards the ephemeral and understated, and the monumentalism that prevails to the East – in Russia, Turkmenistan and, beyond that, in China and the Far East, where giant statues of Buddha and Mao continue to rise… Meanwhile, there is talk of a Museum of Totalitarianism, though there is little consensus within the Ukrainian establishment on the matter. Some view it as an opportunity to educate current and future generations about Communism and its legacy and to promote civil education. Others, like historian Olha Kovalevska, a native of Donetsk, liken the removal of Communist-era monuments to an act of autotomy – where an animal under threat discards part of its body. Ukraine, like a lizard, sheds its tail to escape the totalitarian past. There is no educational value in museifying this appendage, which would only 'serve the needs of moneyed tourists'.

Until then, the scattered Lenins captured here *are* that Museum, a monument to monuments.

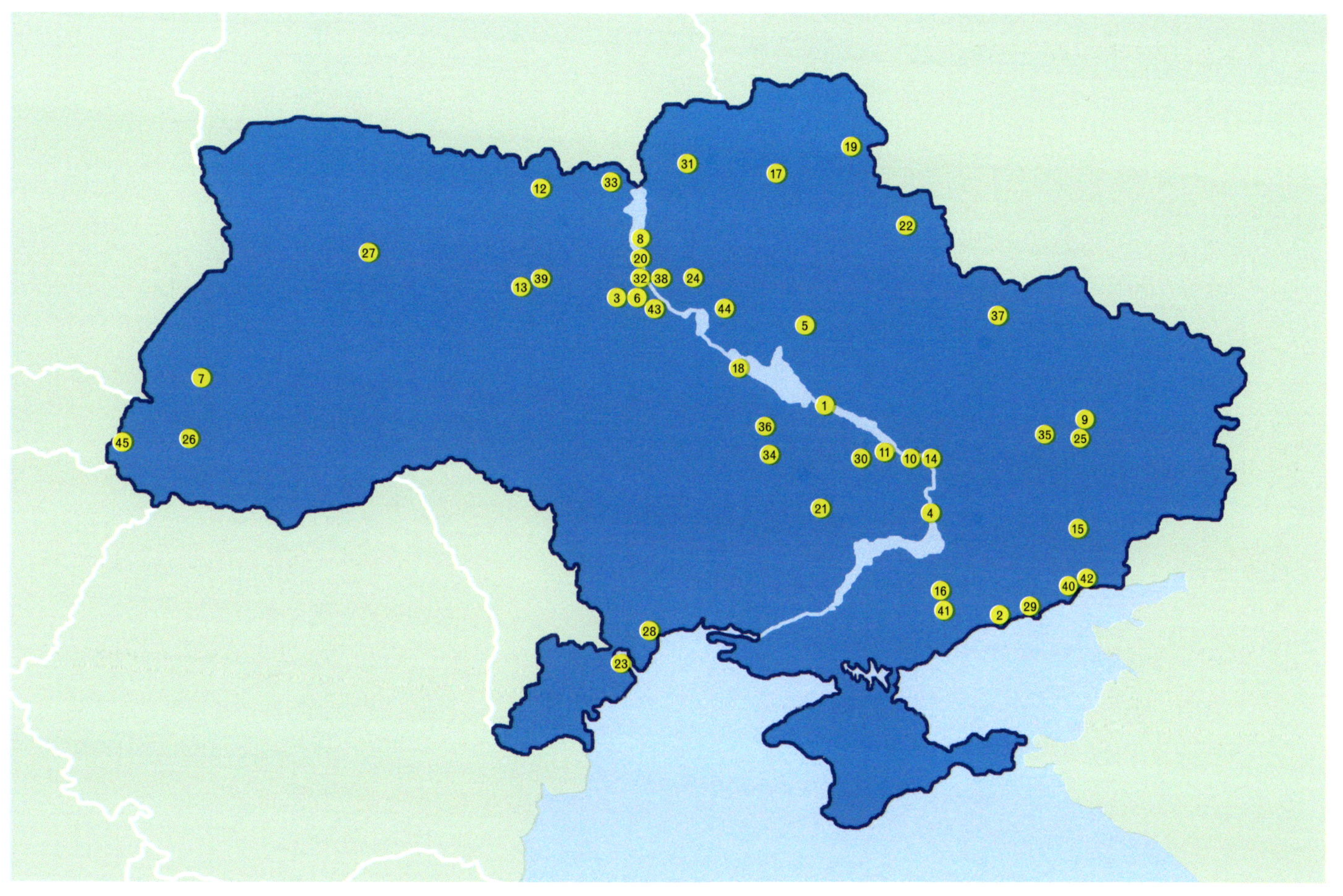

17

LOOK ING FOR LENIN

LOST IN DECOMMUNISATION

NIELS ACKERMANN   SÉBASTIEN GOBERT

Kremenchuk. 30 March 2016

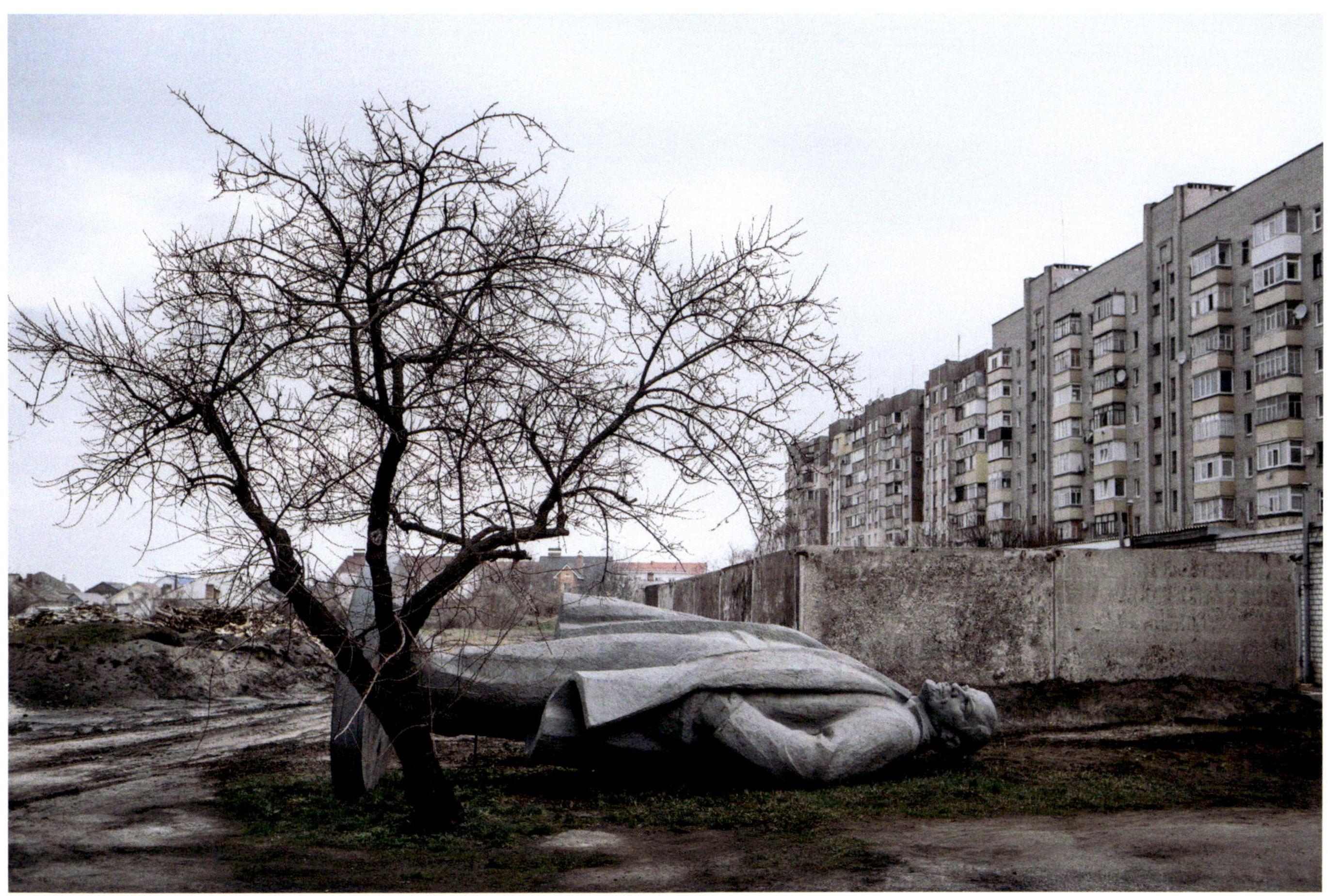

Primorsk. 30 September 2016

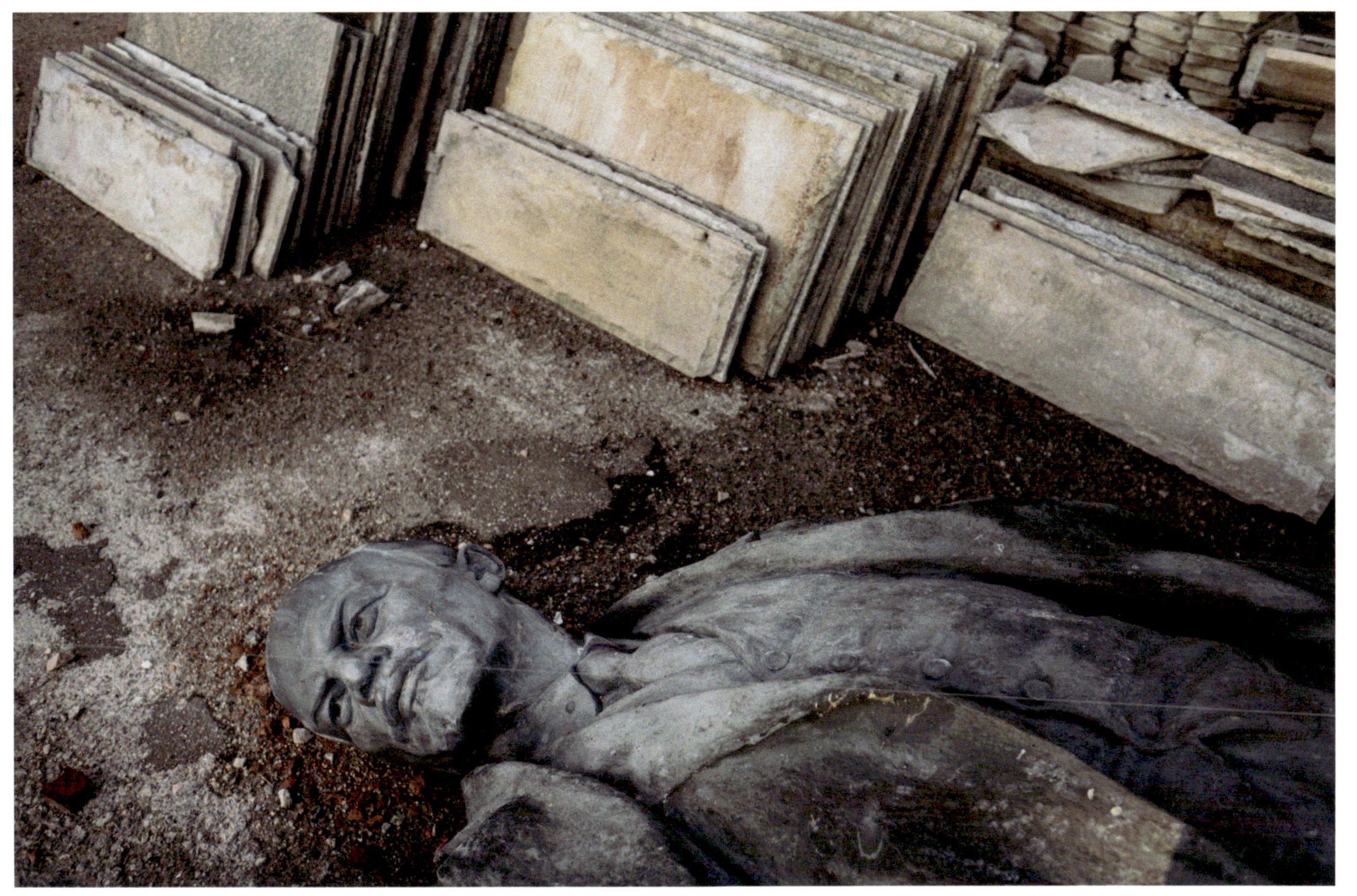

Beheaded Lenin statue exhibited in Kyiv.
Museum of Soviet Occupation, Kyiv. 12 September 2015

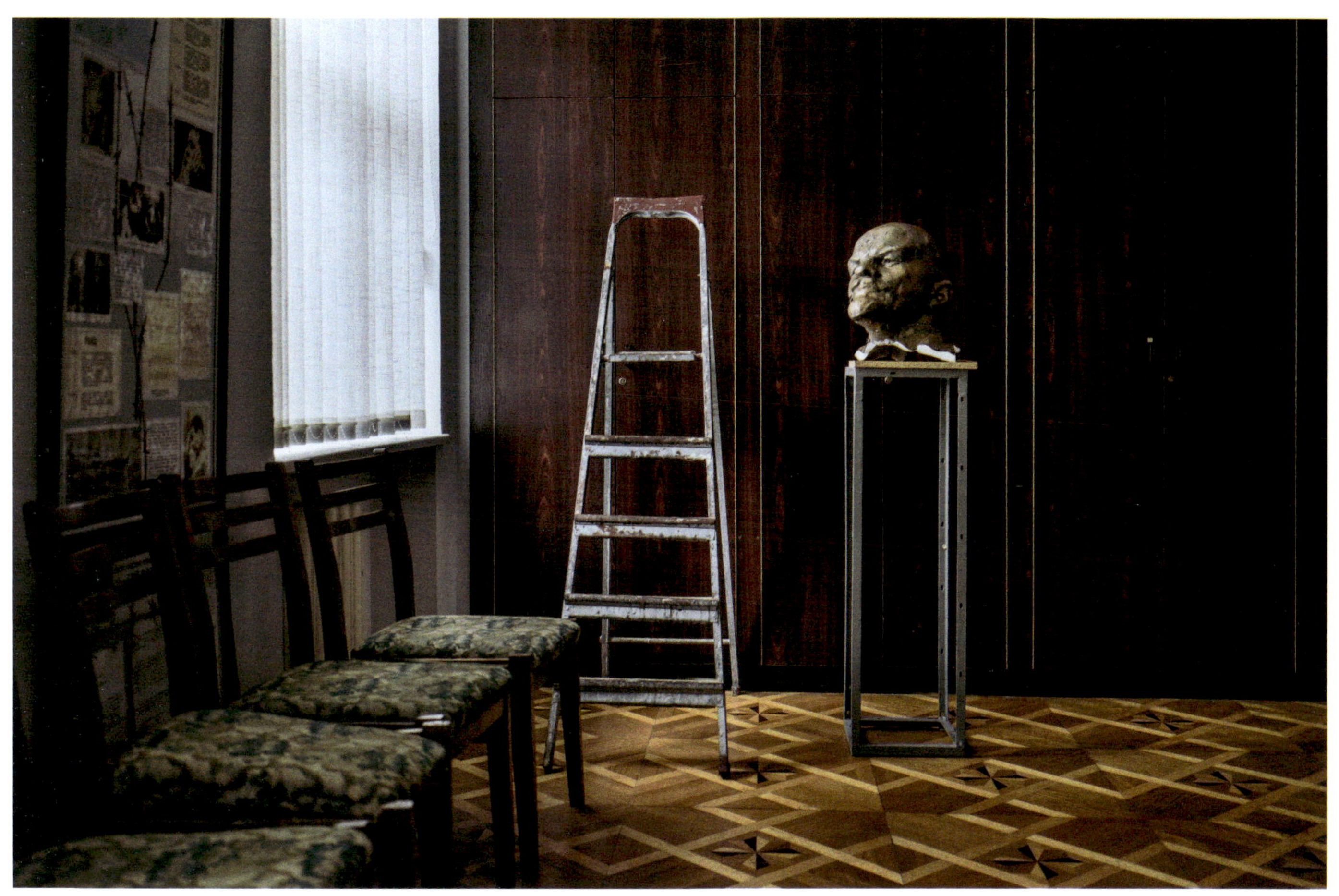

Zaporizhia. 25 July 2016

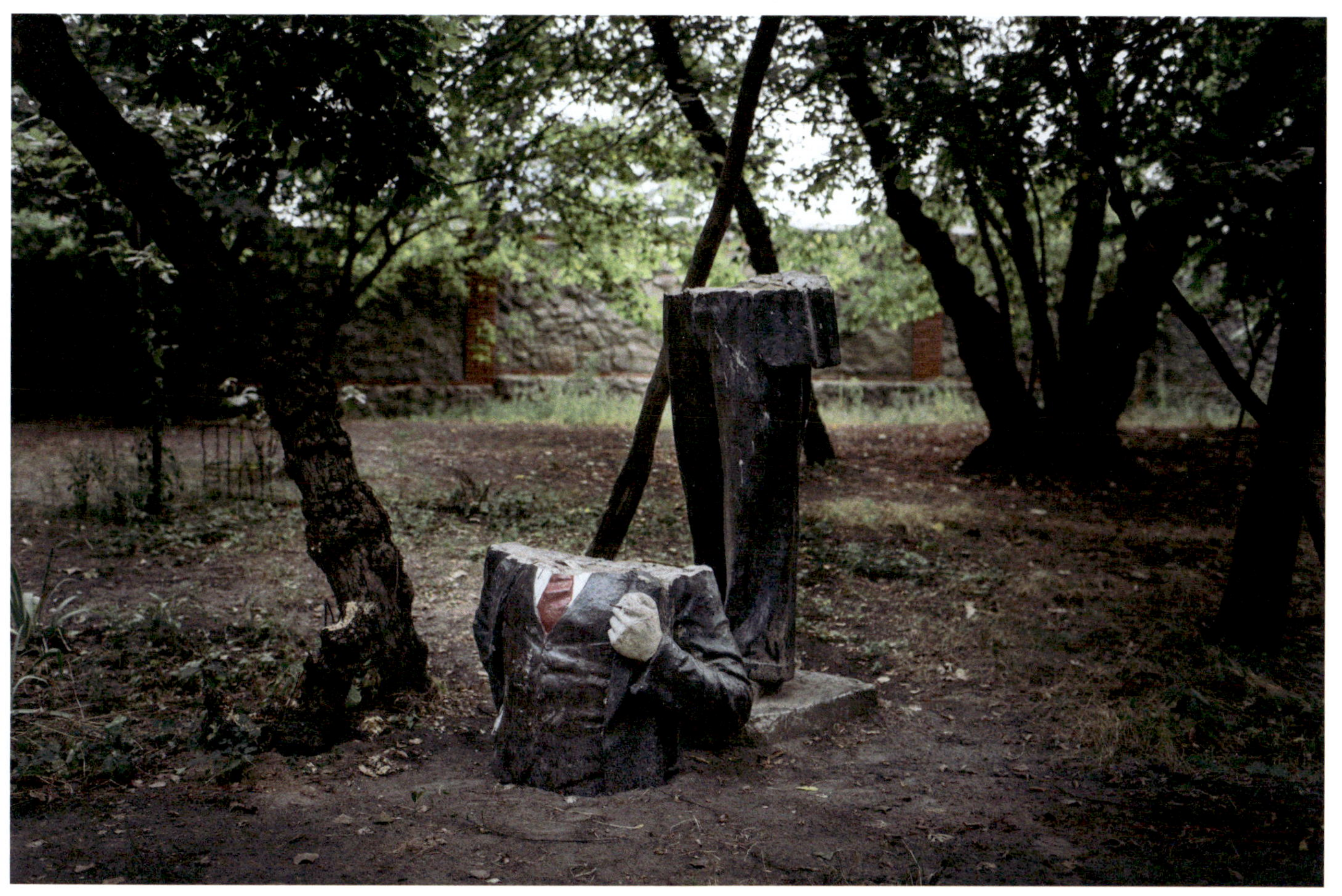

Pokrovska Bahachka, Poltava Region. 13 August 2016

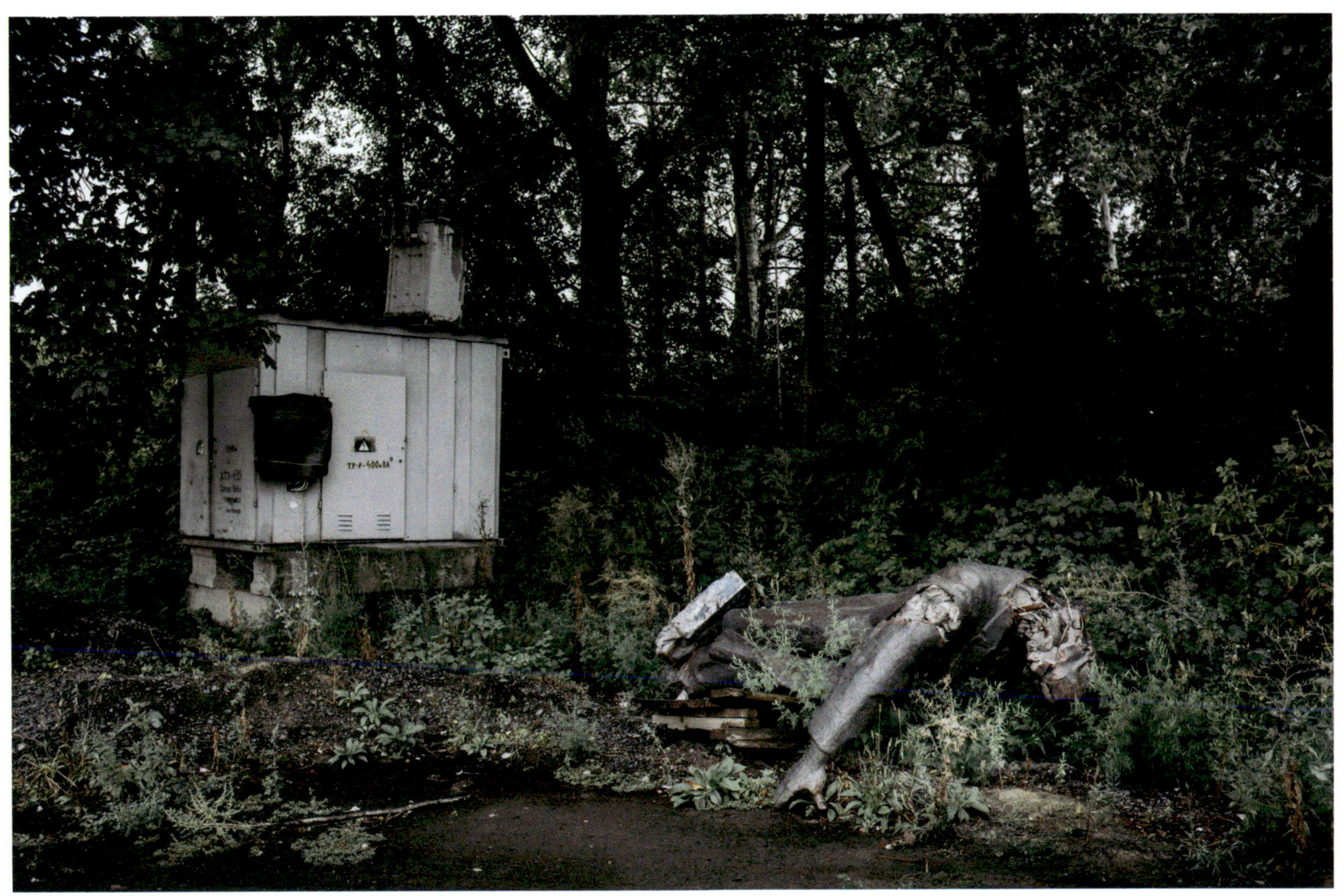

Ukraine National Art Museum, Kyiv. 10 March 2016

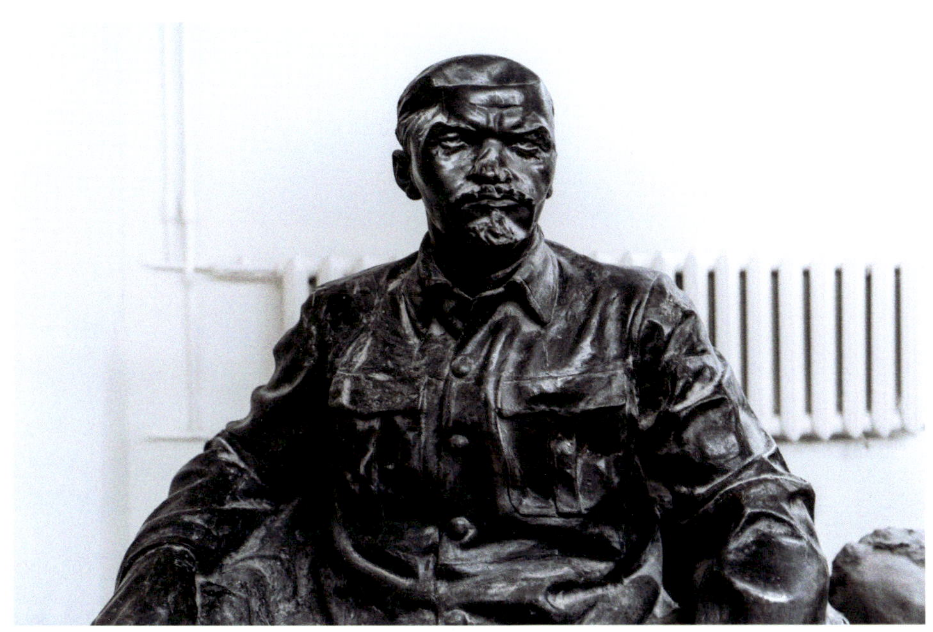

Ukraine National Art Museum, Kyiv. 10 March 2016

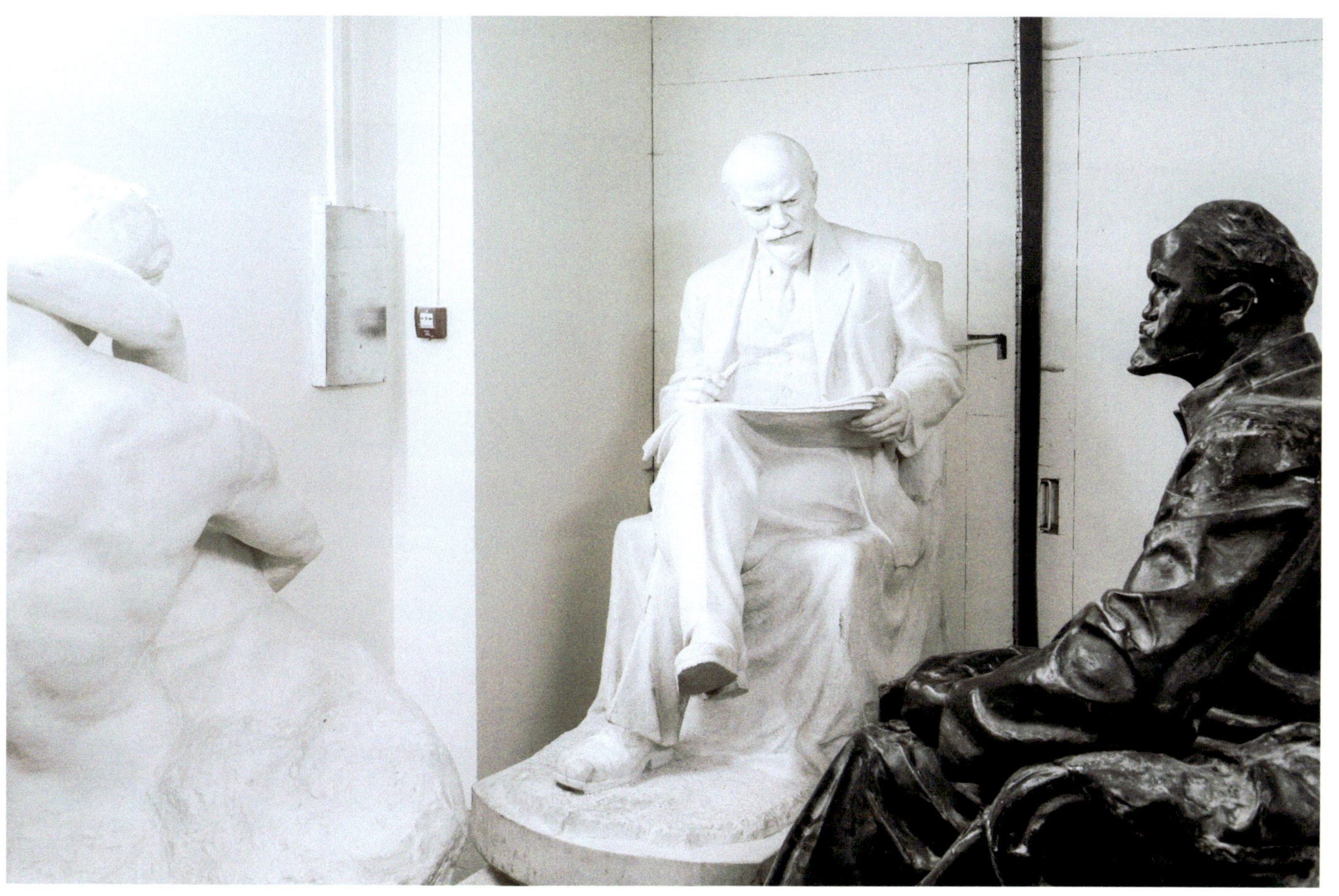

They should have left it there… It belongs to the city landscape and it's part of our history. And now it's here, in the middle of a garbage dump. I'm a former policeman. For many years I was responsible for this district [the left bank of Zaporizhia]. Now, my pension is so low that I have to keep working here as a security guard for the city. And now, here I am, watching over Lenin! What an irony… At least here, they did it in a civilised way, with a crane. But still… You noticed that I was quite strict, right? This is normal. I didn't know who you were. People try to get in here. The Lenin, you know… It's made of bronze, about 40 tonnes worth. I'm not sure of the price per kilo, but it's at least 1000 hryvnias [around 31 euros]. So, you work it out. I watch over it because so many people want to steal the bronze. It belongs to the city. I'm sure they want to sell it too. It'll be good for the budget, unless someone makes the money disappear again… That's it. Our history will disappear, sold for a few dollars…

Oleksandr Oleksievych
Security guard, Zaporizhia

It's quite difficult for me to agree with their decommunisation. It's an important part of our past. Our children have to know about it and to understand what happened in the past — the history of World War II, of course, but also the reasons why the Communists came to power. We have to remember why our Dyadya Lenin [Uncle Lenin] came to power. Of course, this is only my opinion…

Dmytro
City employee, Kremenchuk

Lenin? Ah! You, foreigners, you're all the same! Can't you focus on something really important? Why does this guy fascinate you so much? He symbolises the repression and martyrdom of millions. No one looks for fallen statues of Hitler in Germany! I'm from Lviv, in the West of Ukraine. Back there, we took down the statues of Lenin a long, long time ago. And everything is going well – people are looking towards the future, not the past. The same will happen here. No one cares about Lenin now, because life is so tough. Don't you want to focus on real issues?

'Halyna'
Press officer, City Administration, Zaporizhia

Myself and two colleagues bought this wooden house from the local trade union. We started renovations to save it, and turn it into a hotel. We broke down some false walls in the attic to open up the space. And there they were, behind one of these walls. Two busts of Lenin and one tiny statue. I assume a trade union guy had put them here to save them. Maybe for himself. Maybe he was expecting the Soviets to come back… Anyway, it means that they have been sitting there for over twenty years, because all Soviet monuments disappeared very early across Western Ukraine. Look at them. All tarnished and covered with dust. I have to confess that when we found them, I was afraid for a moment. I didn't know what it was, it seemed dangerous. No one expected to see Lenin here again… Now, I'm no longer afraid, I think it's just fun. But still, I have no idea what to do with them…

Vitaliy
Businessman, Truskavets

These two busts of Lenin were hidden behind a wall by the previous occupiers of the house, twenty-five
years ago. They were discovered during recent renovation works.
Truskavets. 2 November 2016

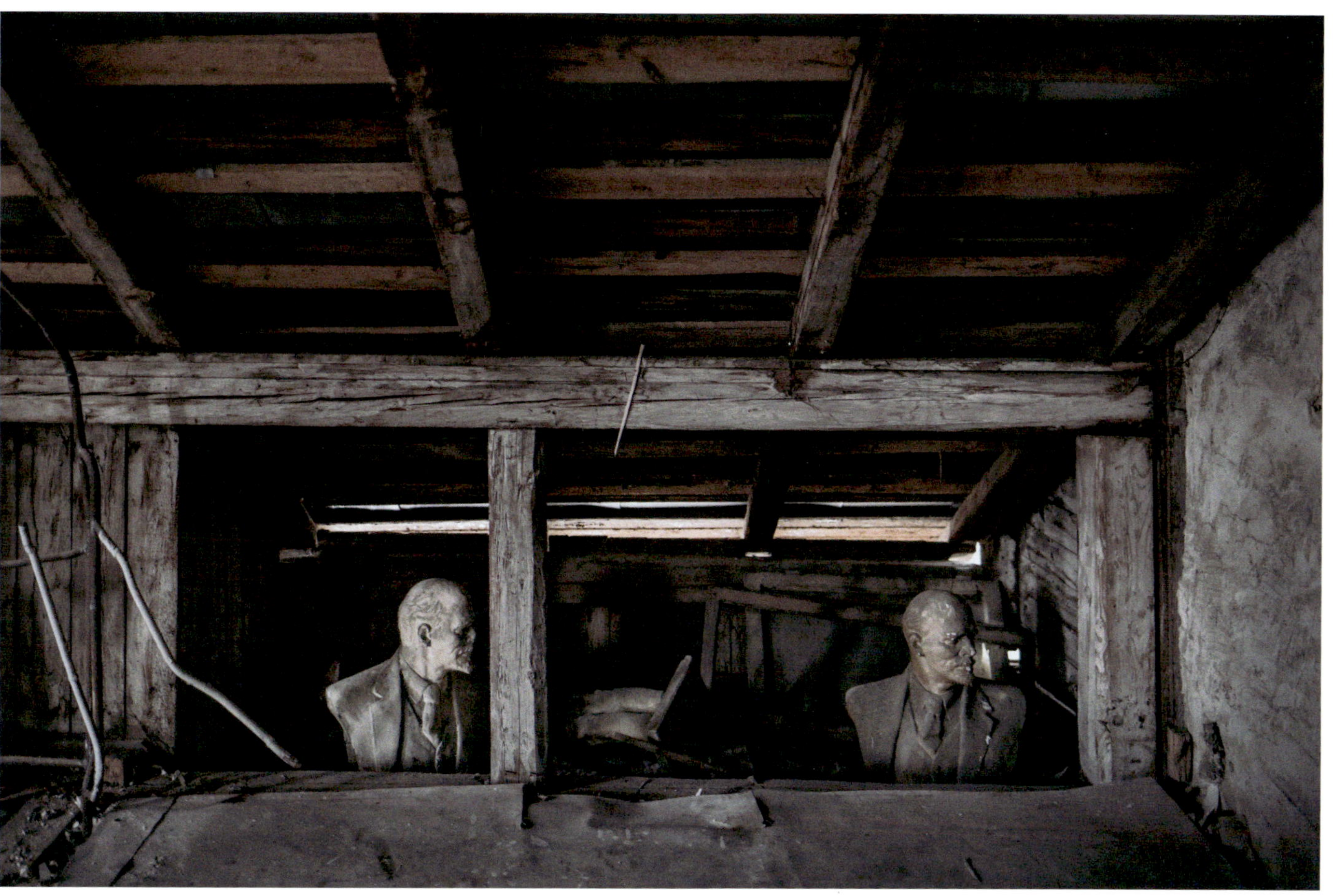

Ukrainian House (former Lenin Museum), Kyiv. 12 January 2016

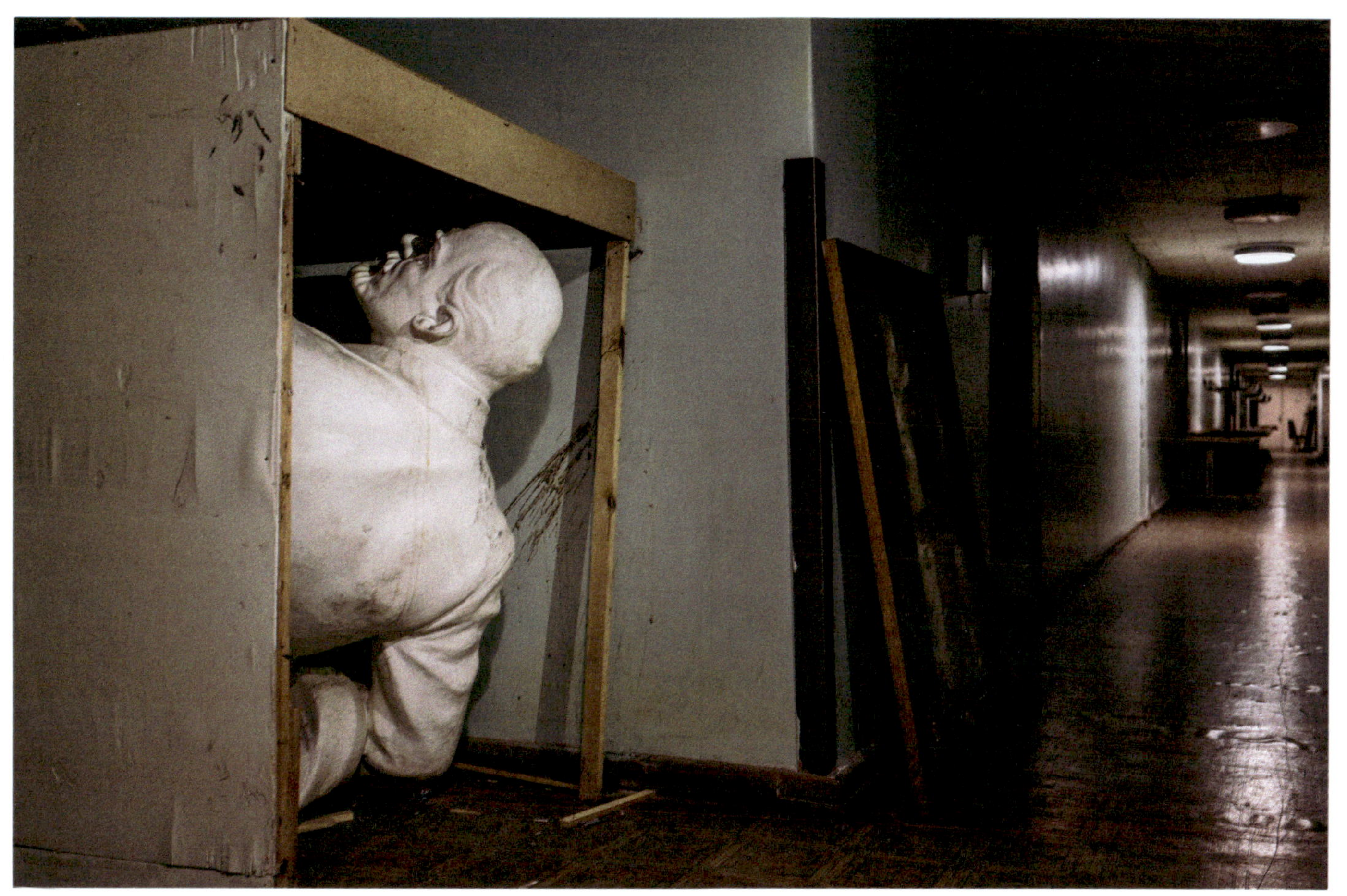

Slovyansk. 15 September 2015

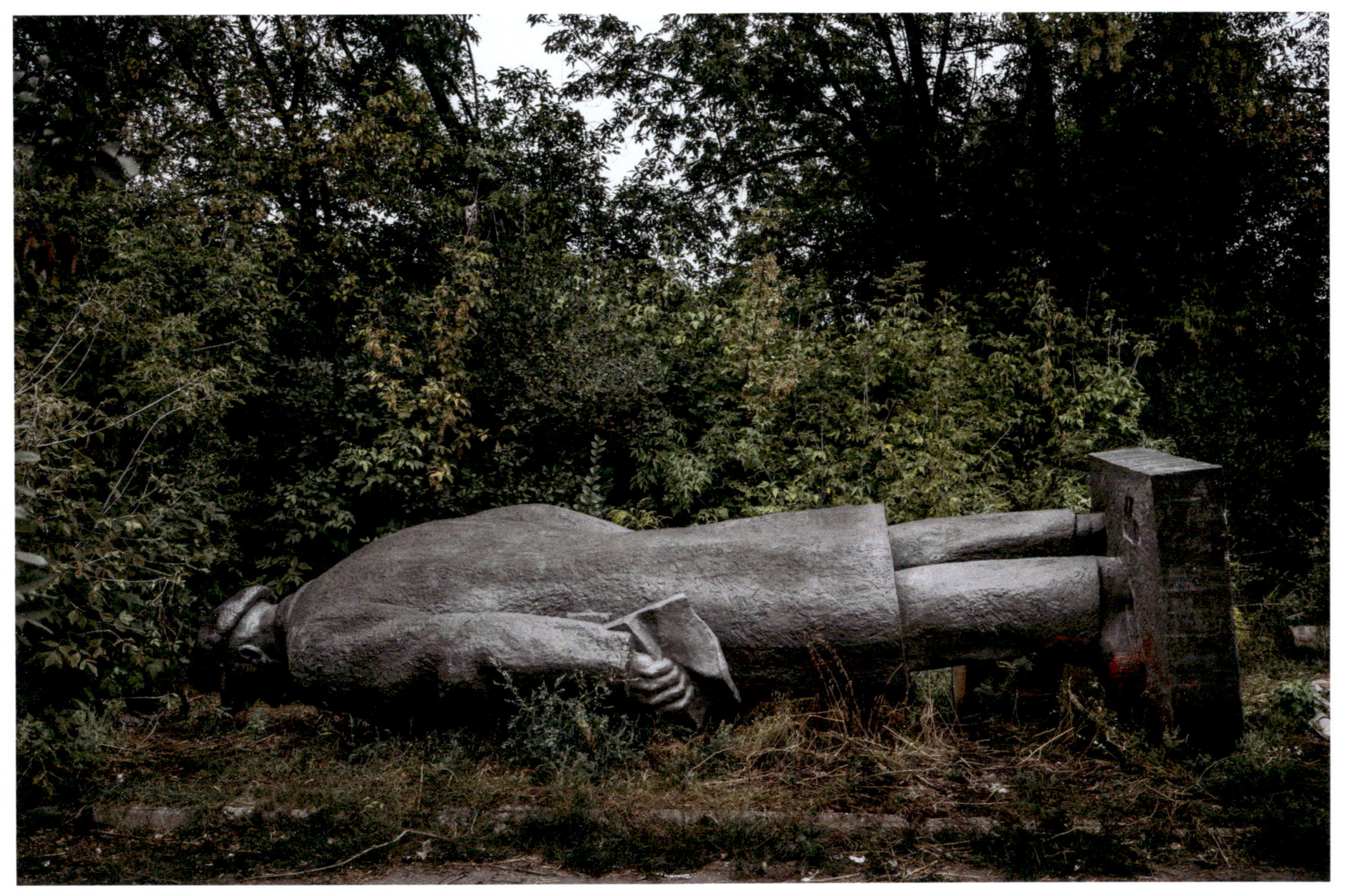

Dniprodzerzhinsk (now Kamianske). 26 July 2016

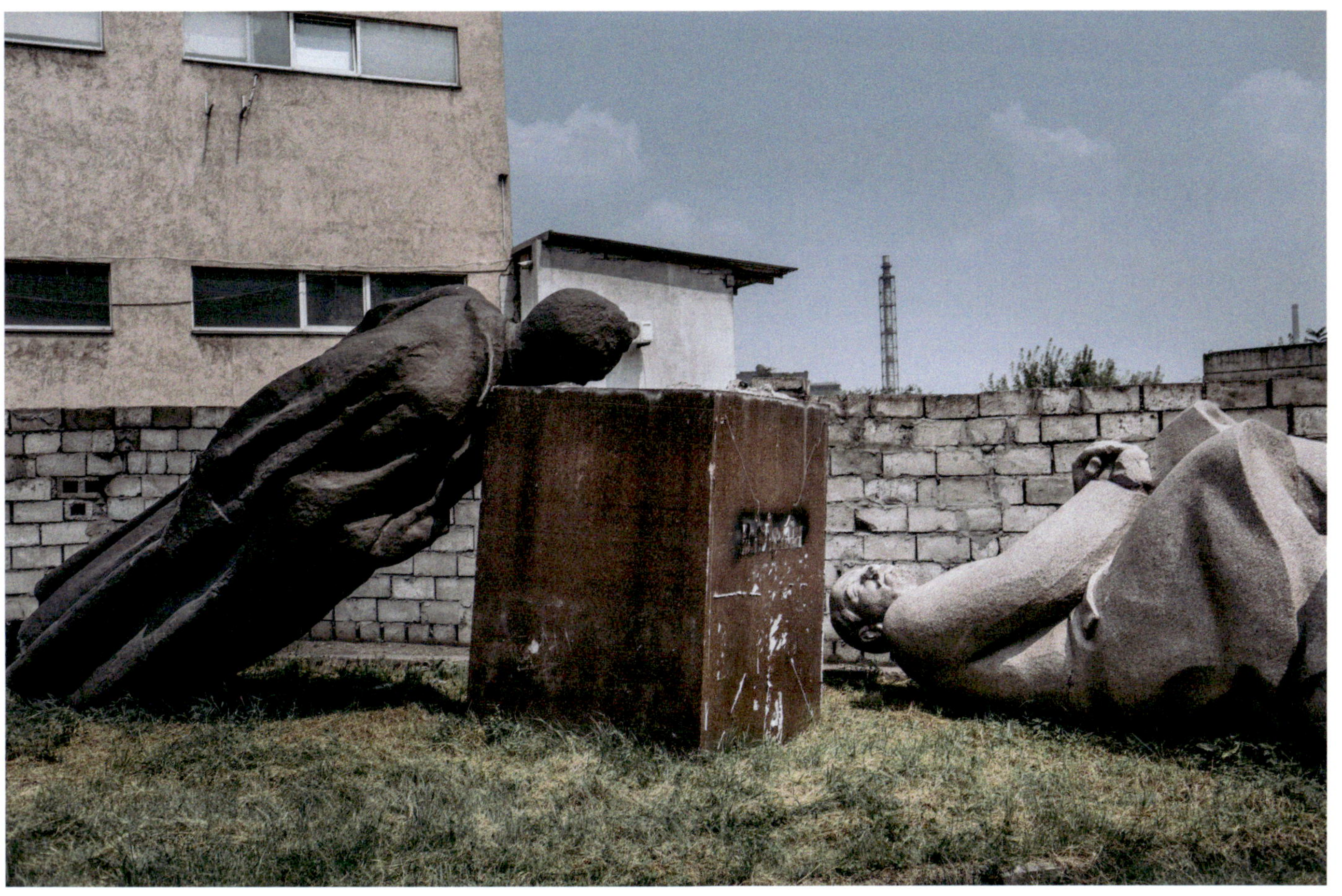

The volunteers of Army SOS, an organisation that helps Ukrainian soldiers in Donbass, were given this bust of Lenin. It stands in their office, surrounded by material ready to be delivered to the frontline. Dnipropetrovsk (now Dnipro). 26 July 2016

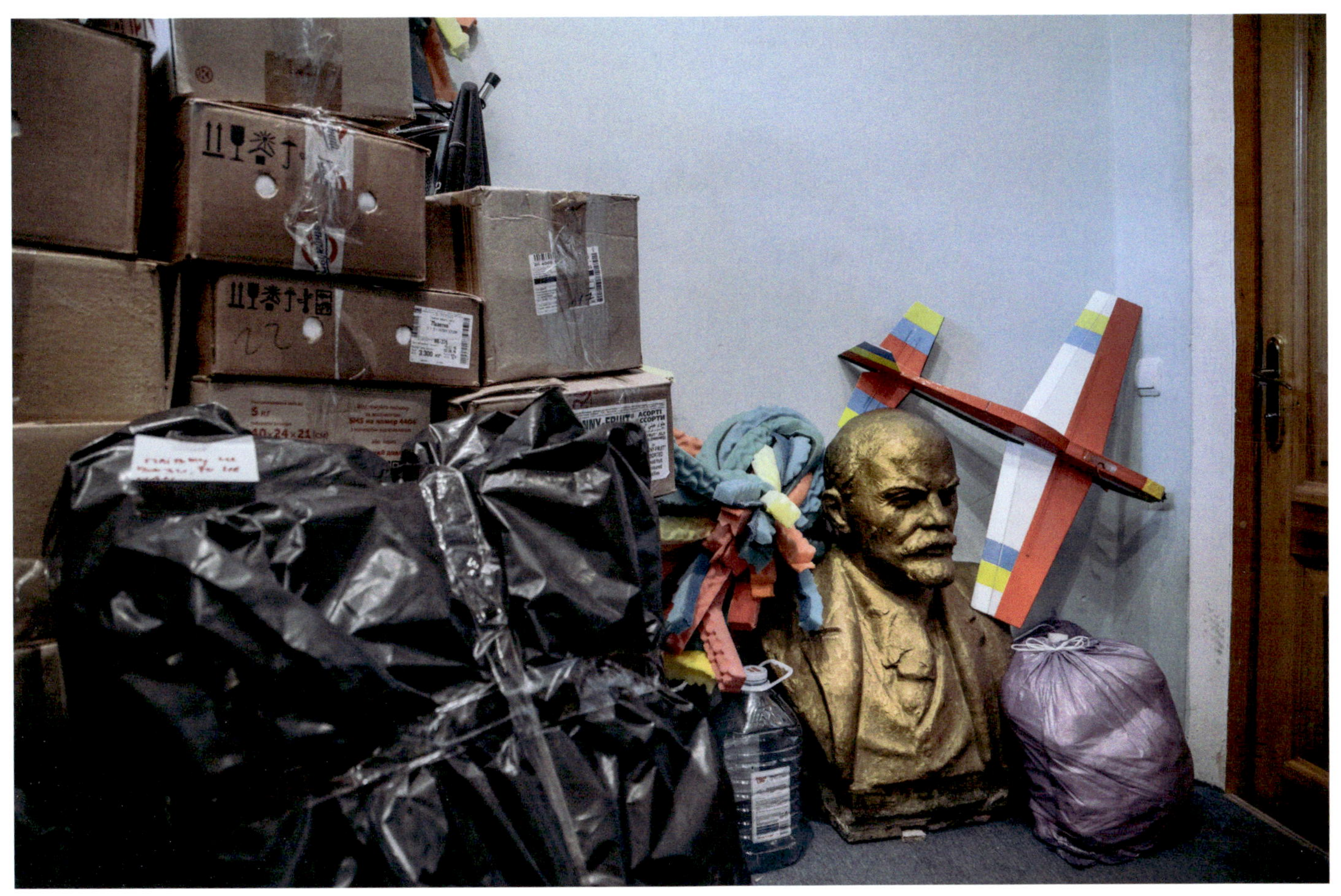

Lasky. 1 July 2016

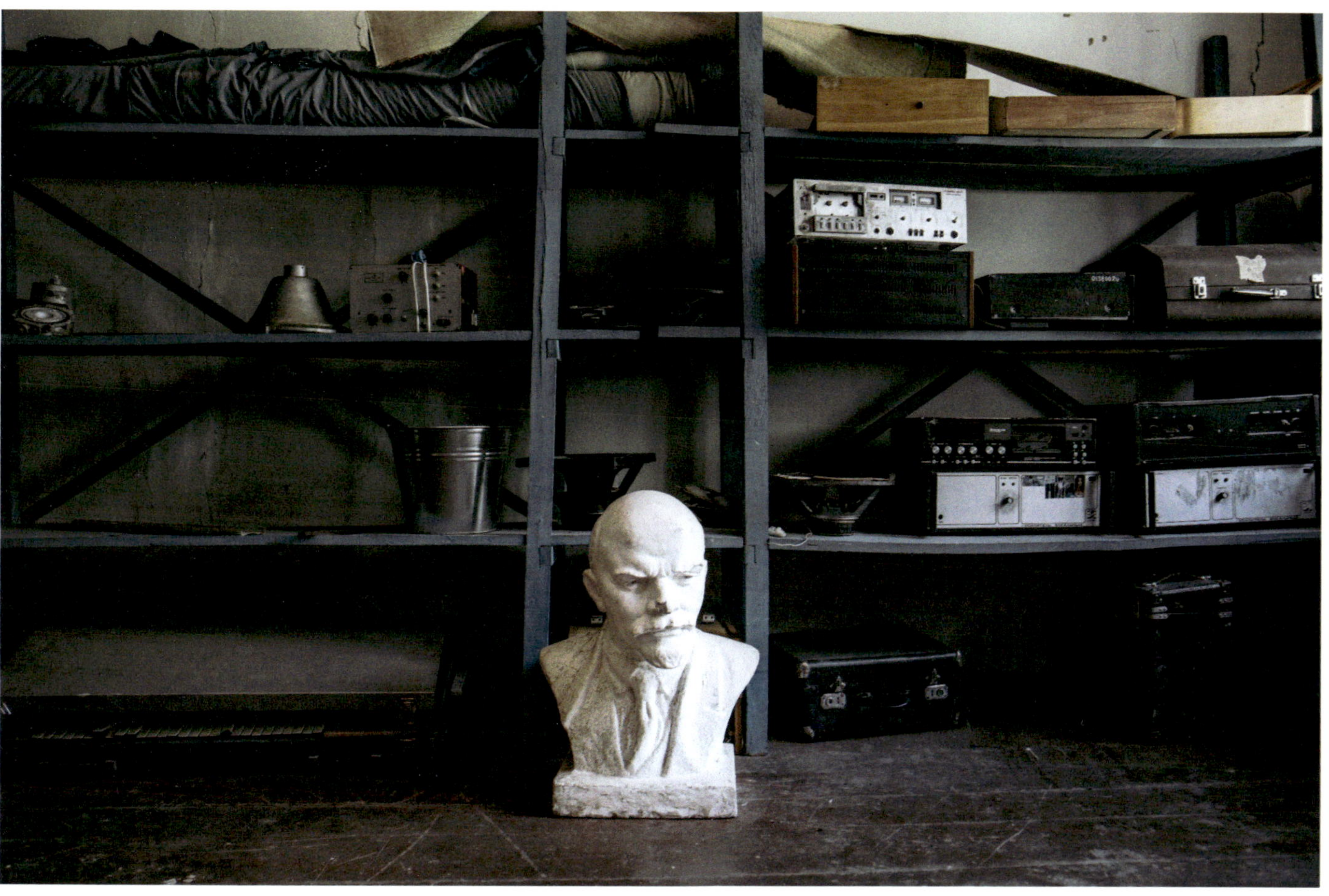

It's a terrible history we have to get rid of. Imagine that a man breaks into your house. He wrecks everything, beats you up, marries your wife and raises your kids. He hangs his portrait on the wall and lives in your shoes. Eventually, the time comes when you are able to take the portrait down – but your own children stop you from doing it! It's part of history, they say… It's absurd. My grandfather fought hard against Soviet colonisation and he was labelled as a dangerous, blood-thirsty fascist because of that. All he did was to protect his family and his fatherland against foreign aggression. And look now, it is happening again! Soviets, Russians, it's all the same. They're just different expressions of this imperial spirit. I recently appeared on TV with a man from Eastern Ukraine. He told me that he'd grown up thinking all Western Ukrainians were fascists. But when he realised what the Russians are doing in Donbass, he accepted that we were right to fight against Russians. He told me he doesn't want to hear about Lenin any more.

Yuriy Shukhevych
Member of Parliament, Lviv [Son of Roman Shukhevych, General of the
Ukrainian Insurgent Army]

Decommunisation is fear. It happens because of fear. People are scared of their past, dissatisfied with their present and anxious about their future. So they take monuments down. But I don't believe you can blame the monuments for what has happened in the past! On the contrary: these statues are now a part of our history, whether we like it or not. Yet still, they want to break them down. I find it quite sad. Another thing that saddens me is the emptiness afterwards. History teaches us that such radical action – the tearing down of an ideology – is usually followed by the assertion of a new one. Not in Ukraine. Nothing comes next, at least I don't see it. Look at Bessarabska Square. It's been over two years since they took that Lenin down. And now? The pedestal with the name 'Lenin' on it still stands. Nothing else. More than two years! I would like to see a park dedicated to storing all these fallen monuments, which are part of our history. It would attract tourists and bring money. At least that would be positive. But I don't see anyone planning it.

Lyudmila
Kyiv History Museum, Kyiv

So! You came here just to see this? Go on, take a good look! Take a look at the mess we have in this country! There is no respect for anything now. What do you mean, where is the head? They cut it off and took it away! I've no idea where it went! They did it at night. When we woke up, Lenin had no head. And no one does anything about it. We grew up with Lenin, for God's sake! I lay flowers at his feet every 1 May [International Workers' Day in the former Soviet Union]. Our school was beautiful on that day, full of colour. Once we graduated, we had jobs waiting for us, just like that! Today everything gets worse and worse. Look, look! They went sadistic on him, painting him and all... Take a good look! The roads are all potholed, the façades are falling apart, young people leave the village to find a better future in the city. And these guys, they just want to destroy Lenin. It's not going to change anything, is it? I know, the things he did, Vladimir Ilyich... Whatever. Look at our statue, our nice golden statue. It was part of the village, it used to make us proud! And now, you came from France, and you want to take a picture of this. You are going to show it on the internet, aren't you? On Facebook, or whatever it's called. Everyone is going to laugh at us. It's a shame, what they do to us! Everyone will laugh and mock us. After that, they'll forget us, once again...

'Babushka' (grandmother)
Shabo

Of course Lenin must go. He was a dictator who caused the death of millions of Ukrainians. The Ukrainian People's Republic, formed in 1919, was the true expression of the Ukrainian nation's will. What came after was nothing less than invasion and occupation. You know what came after: purges, the Holodomor – the great famine in 1932-33 – more purges, more suffering... Of all the people in the USSR, Ukrainians suffered the most during the Second World War! The Great Patriotic War, they call it. What patriotism? What motherland? The Soviet Union repressed our national identity and tried to tarnish it as some kind of folk culture. They Russified our land and mocked our language. And they are doing the same again now in Crimea and Donbass. I know people feel nostalgic for the USSR, Lenin, the pioneers... I'm not deaf. I hear the critics against decommunisation. But who are they? People filled with useless paternalism, who miss their youth. They're not important. It's the next generations that we're fighting for. So Lenin has to go. Obviously.

Volodymyr Viatrovych
Director, Ukrainian Institute for National Remembrance, Kyiv

Zhytomyr. 18 November 2015

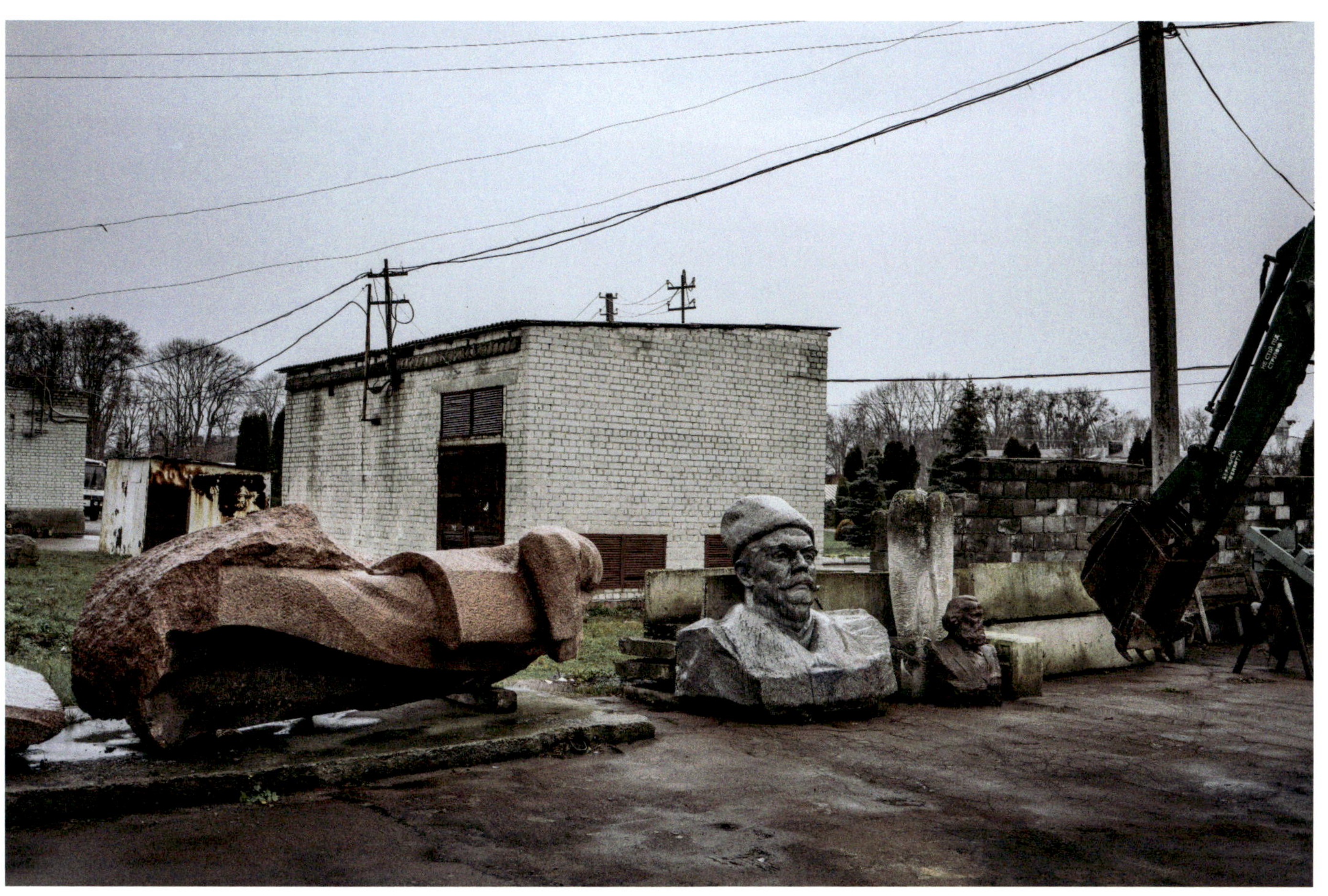

The head of Dnipropetrovsk's Lenin was given to the city's National History Museum. It remains in storage as the institution does not currently have the resources to exhibit it.
Dnipropetrovsk (now Dnipro). 13 November 2015

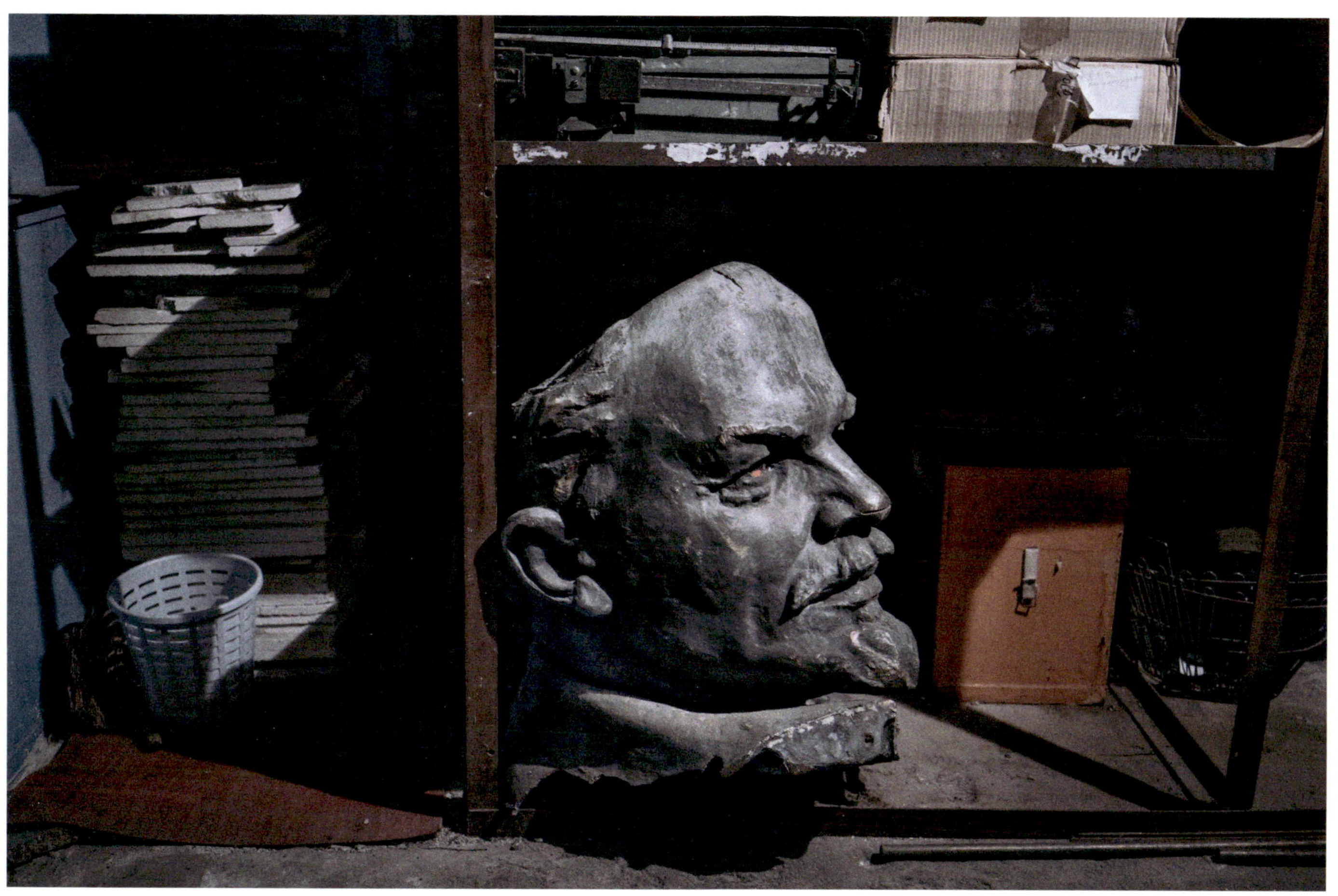

Volnovakha. 1 October 2016

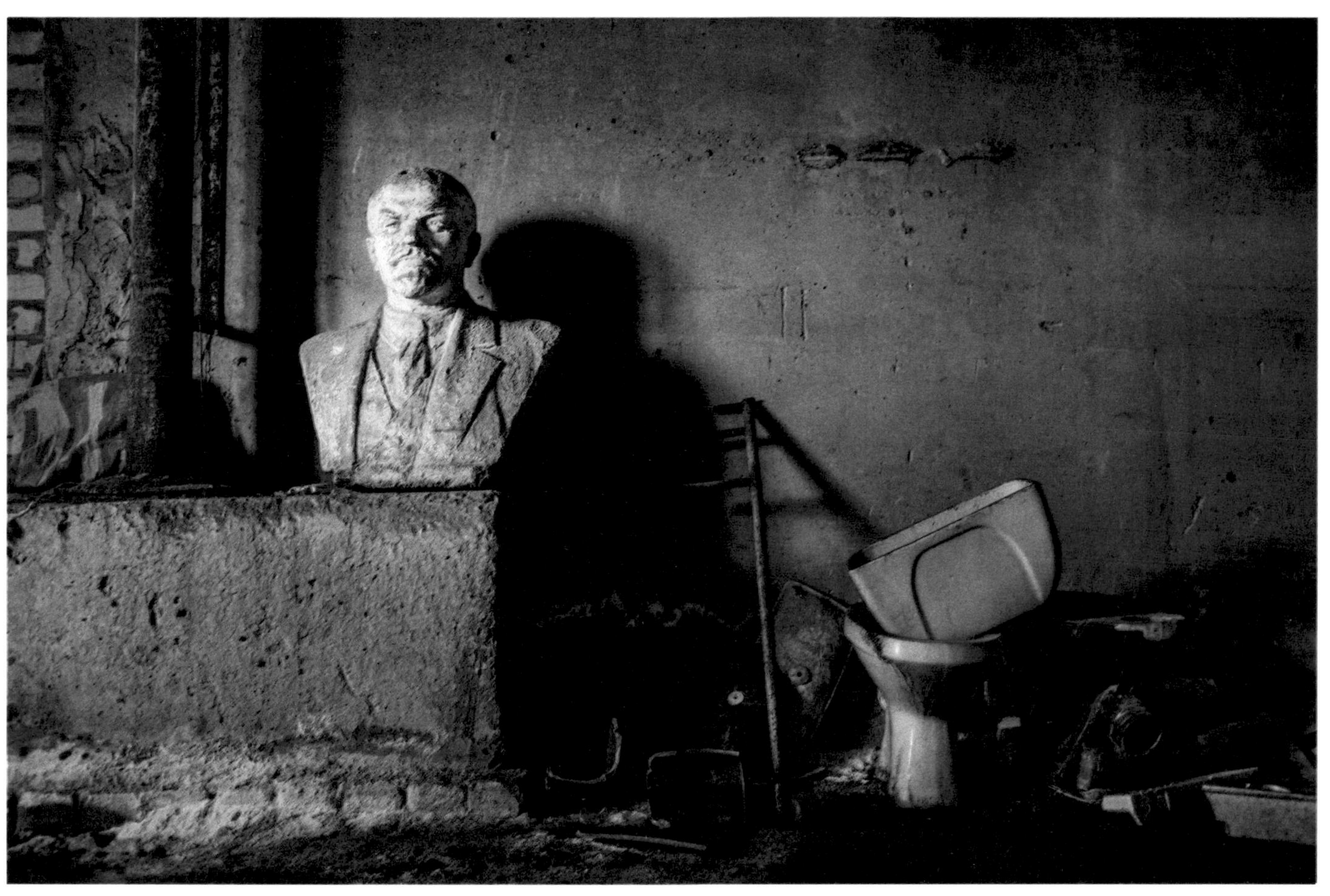

Novobohdanivka. 30 September 2016

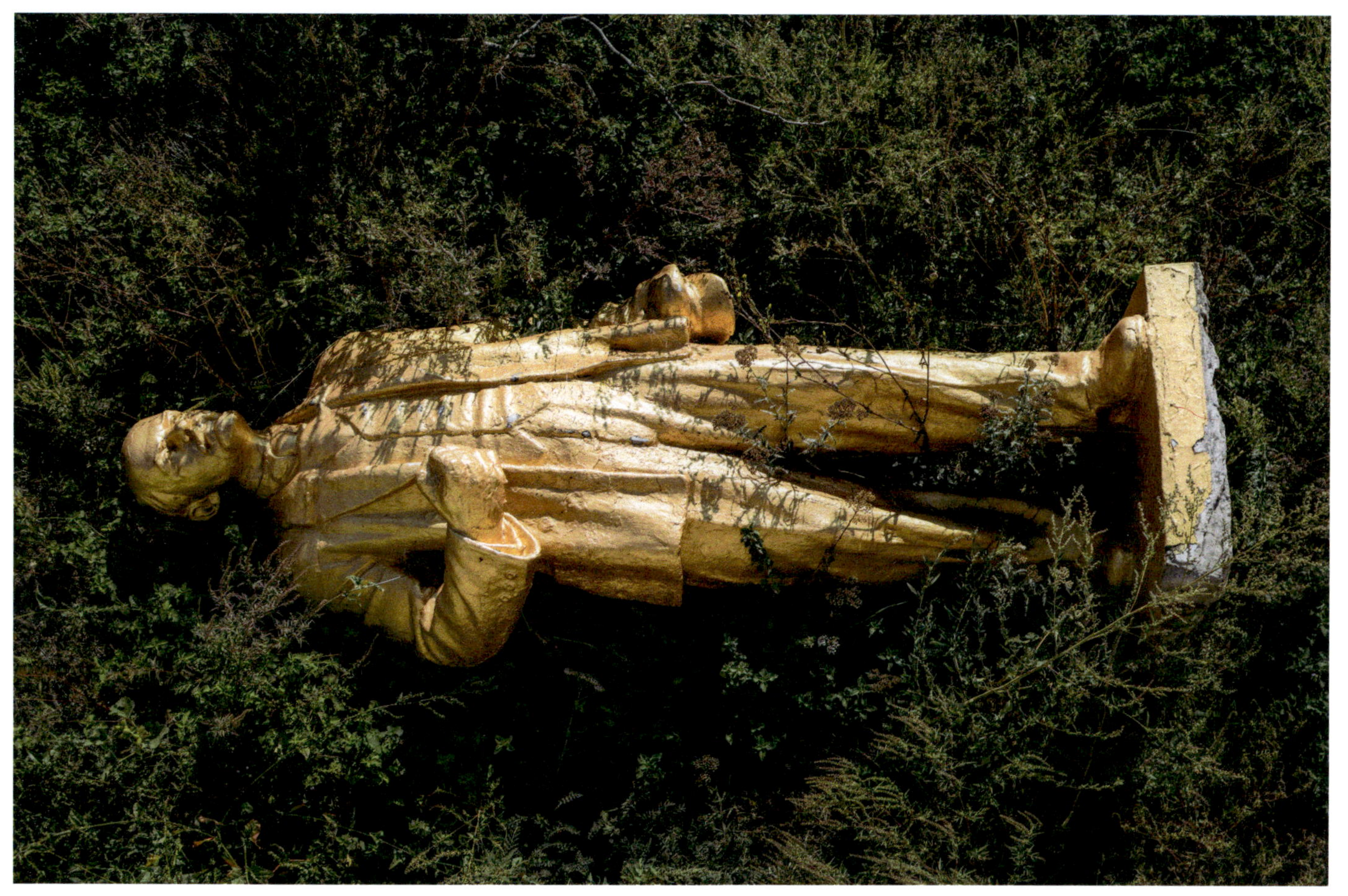

Palats Ilych (Lenin Palace, House of Culture), Dnipropetrovsk (now Dnipro). 24 July 2016

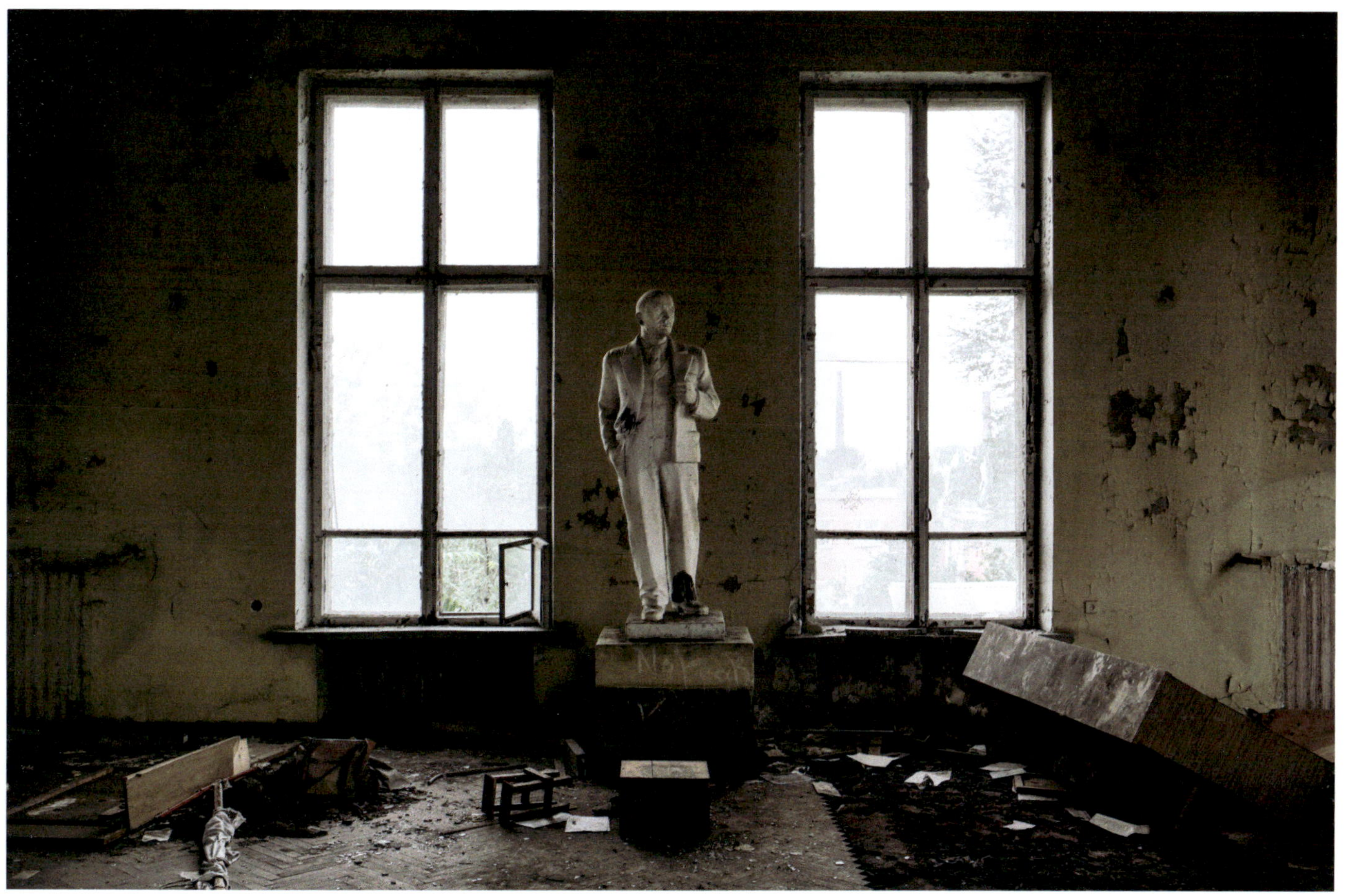

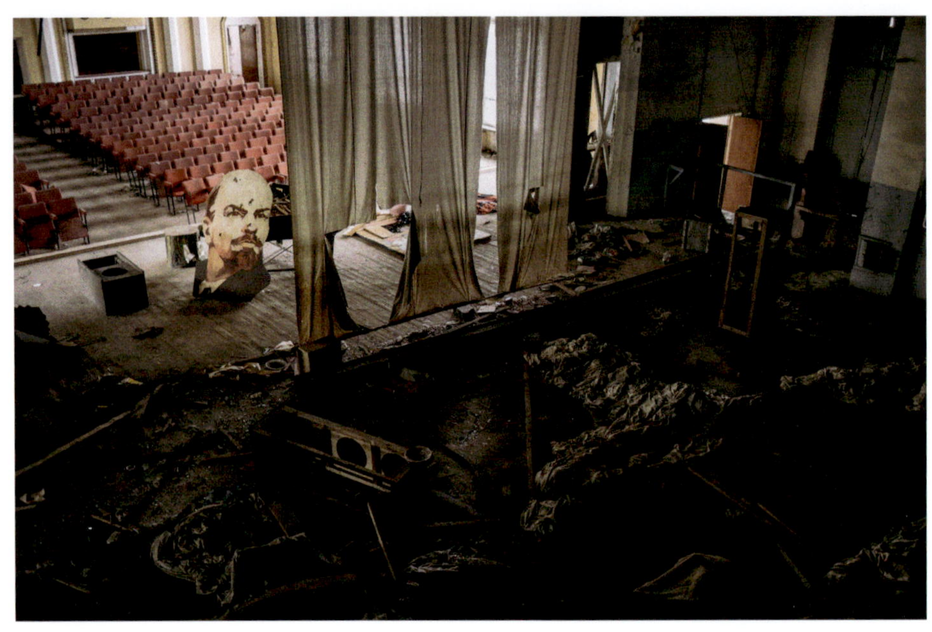

Palats Ilych (Lenin Palace, House of Culture), Dnipropetrovsk (now Dnipro). 24 July 2016

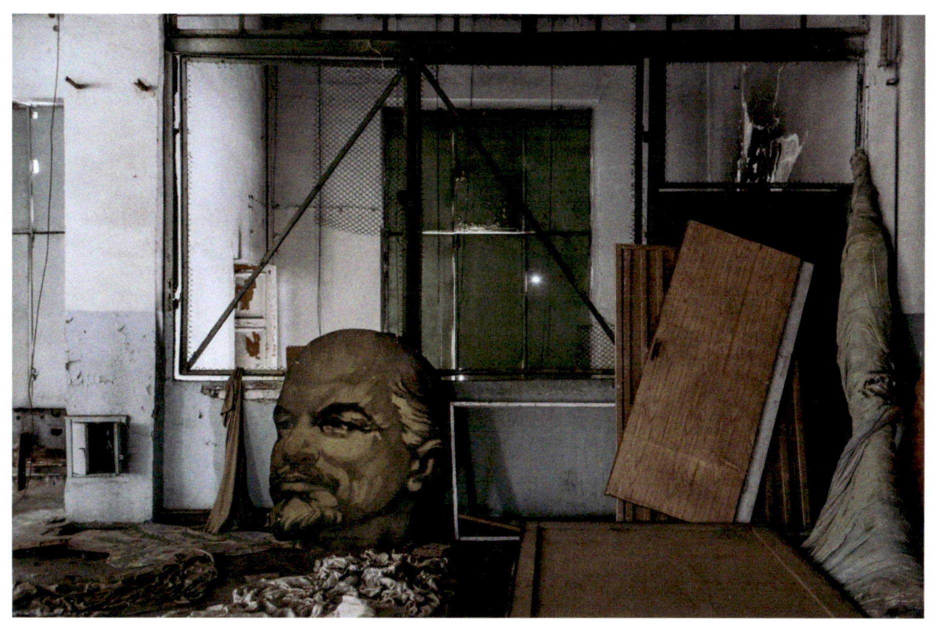

The graffiti, sprayed in the colours of the Ukrainian flag, reads: 'Putin is a dickhead la la la!'
Dnipropetrovsk (now Dnipro). 25 July 2016

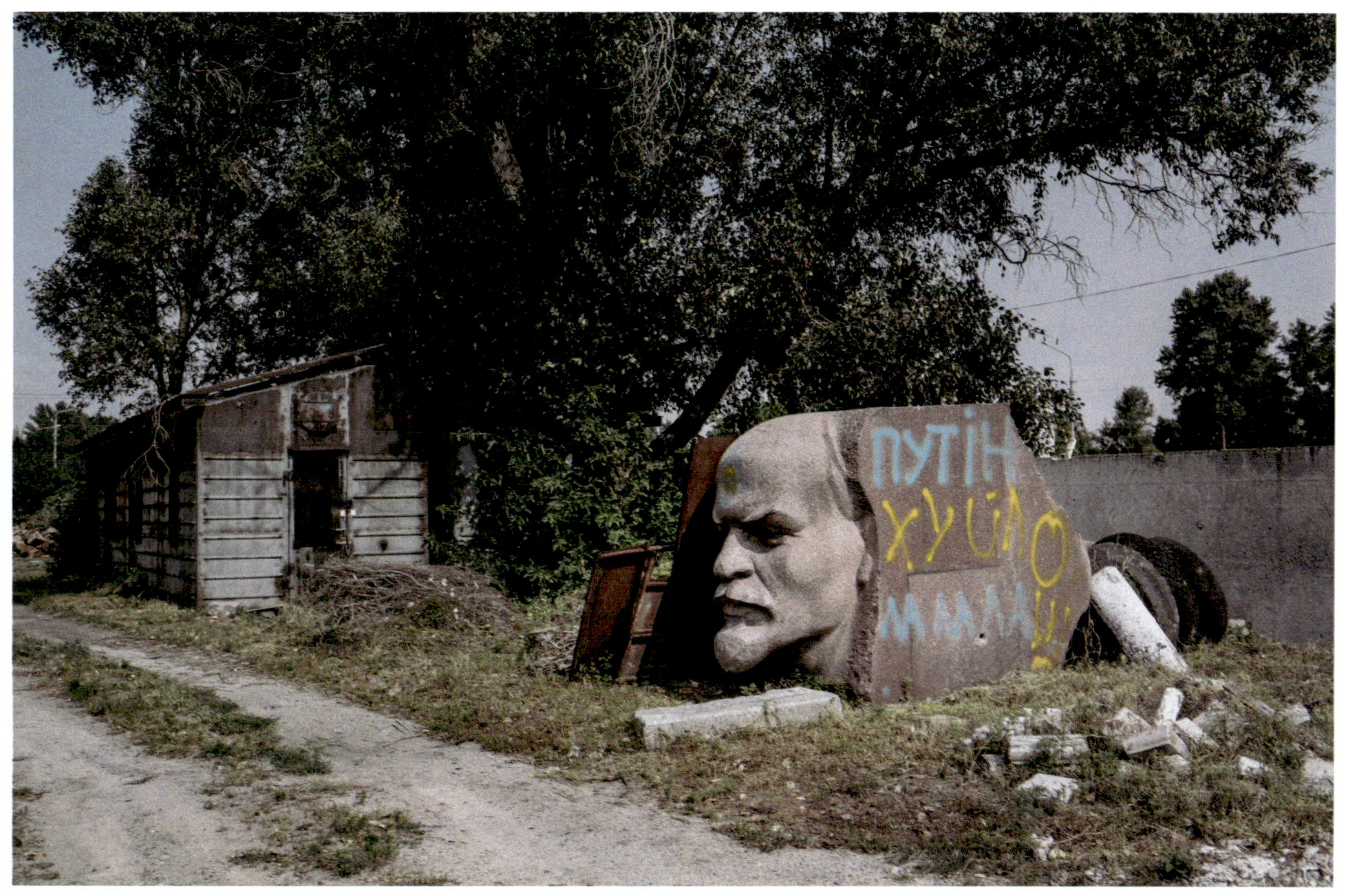
ПУТІН
ХУЙЛО
МАЛА

When it comes to decommunisation and desovietisation in Ukraine, it seems difficult to me to compare Communism with Nazism, as the law states. We all know about the crimes of the Communist regime, many of which were committed on these lands. Yet the Communist era was one of differences. It was harsher during certain periods, softer in others. As it lasted so long, it became normality. Its achievements, in terms of infrastructural or educational policies, for instance, are unquestionable. Even Ukraine's current borders count as one of these achievements. Ukraine may now claim sovereignty over Crimea, only because the Soviet regime transferred the peninsula to Kyiv back in 1954. In my opinion, to base a new national narrative on a polarised vision of history, one that rejects everything that was Soviet, is a dangerous trend – especially at a time of war. It may unify the nation, yet it also antagonises a large part of the population. I don't know if there will be an official protest in many cases when Lenin statues are toppled. We see that the people who disagree do not necessarily voice their dissatisfaction openly. Yet their dissatisfaction is real. It nourishes frustrations that can erupt later in the context of war or elections.

Ioulia Shukan
Lecturer at Paris West University Nanterre La Défense, author of
Génération Maïdan, Paris

If it had stayed in the open air, the pigeons would've shat on it. It would've been damaged by rain. So I took it indoors. It's going to be a part of our *bania* [Russian sauna]. Then people can explain to their grandkids who he was while they bathe. Us Armenians, we like history. We like to learn about history. So I took it. Some people say to me that pigeon shit actually brings good luck and that I should have left the statue outdoors. But for me it's bad luck. So I took it. I don't know what kind of luck Lenin will bring to my business. We will see.

Ashot
Businessman, Volnovakha

No matter how strong and powerful you are, nature will take over. Very soon, within two or three years, you'll see wild plants and vines growing all over. That's why I put these monuments here, in my garden. I hate Lenin, trust me. But I want to show that nature is stronger. It's going to eat them. So it's a living exhibition. When I brought them here they were all the same, different versions of the same form. So me and my kids painted them to make them more fun. They become different and intriguing. I tried to make this spot a kind of mystical place, so you have this Lenin guarding the entrance to the site, this one warning the visitor. This one is more welcoming… Some people advise me that I might bring bad vibrations to my garden with so many Lenins. But I don't think so… I remember the day we brought them in. Shortly after we laid them on the grass, a very strong wind began to blow, then a hail storm started. That day I told myself that I'd provoked bad spirits… But now I feel good on this spot. If you look at history, these statues are how Lenin is remembered: as being the same all the time. But there were periods when Lenin was blood-thirsty, like this. Or frightening, like this. At some point, he was some kind of a funny clown, like this. Here we can think about all these differences. Most importantly, it shows the history of an empire whose fate is to be consumed by nature.

Leonid Kanter
Artist, Obyrok

It took two days for our Lenin to be taken down. Most people were happy with the civilised way it happened, compared to some of the other monuments that were crushed and destroyed. The good thing was that it allowed hundreds to come and say goodbye to Lenin! My office is nearby, so I watched babushkas crying and shouting their love to him. Only then did I realise how badly we'd been brainwashed. I was a pioneer when I was younger – I too, learned poems about Lenin by heart. 'Lenin is always with you, Lenin is always alive,' we used to say… When you find out all the horrible things he and his cronies did in their time… It's scary to think that some people miss this statue. You know, one of their main arguments was that 'the Lenin statue always stood on the main square, so we should keep it that way'. I checked: it was only erected in the 1970s! So there really was no reason to keep it. But now no one knows what to replace it with. It took over a year for them finally to bring it down – that still wasn't long enough to think what to put there instead. There are a few crazy ideas: a monument to gardeners? To cats? Even to cosmonauts! No one has really thought about what it would mean for the city, for our collective identity. Since Zaporizhia is the home to the Cossack Sich, why not a monument to Cossacks? One nationalist guy has proposed such a statue, but it's huge and super kitsch! I am part of a group that discusses and develops local urban projects, flower beds and stuff like that. I am always surprised that the only thing local residents care about at the meetings are the aesthetics. It has to be beautiful. Even if it's out of place in their neighbourhood, even if it has no meaning for them.

Natasha Lobach
Architect, Zaporizhia

Zaporizhia. 31 March 2016

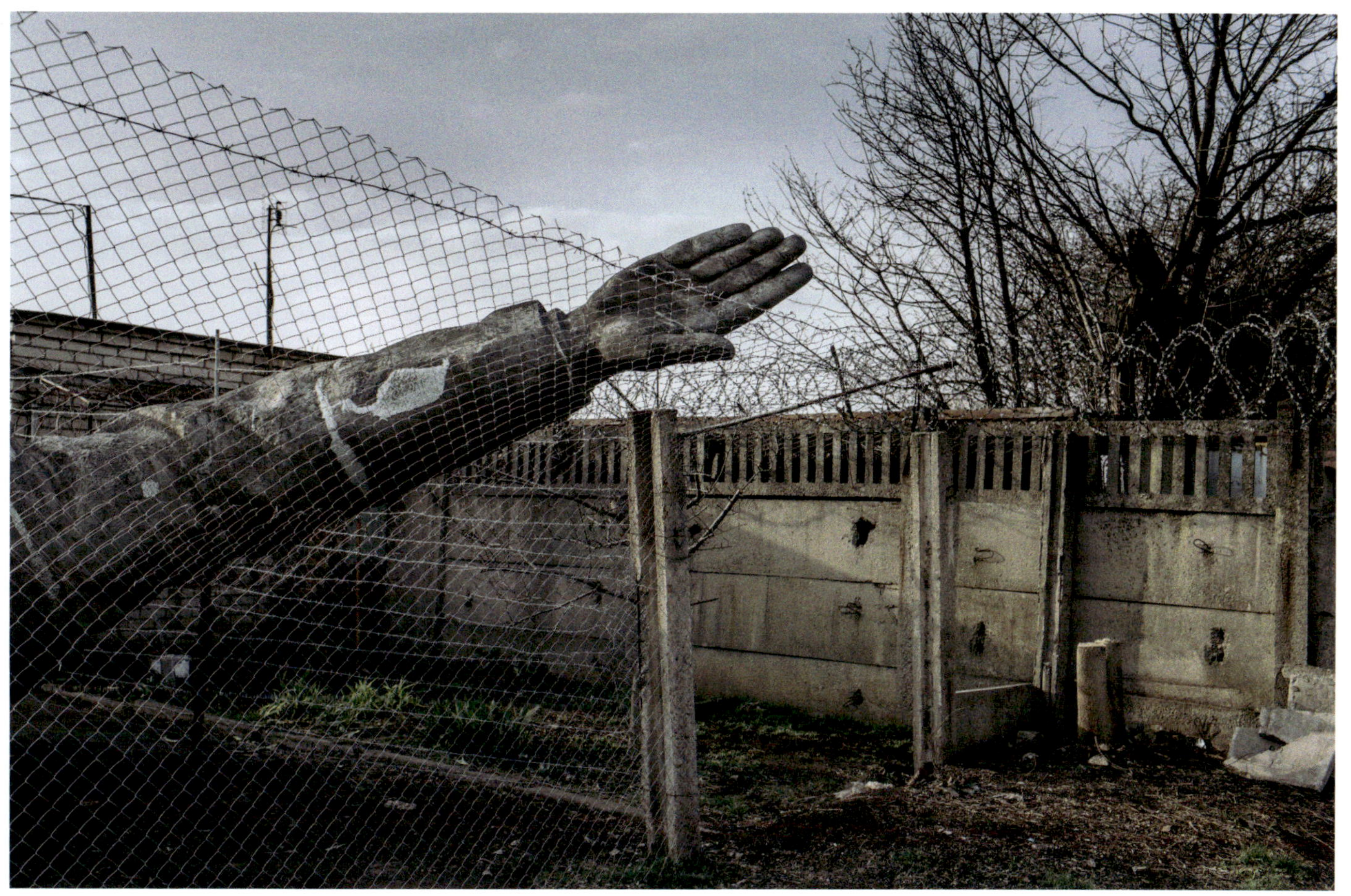

Artist Leonid Kanter owns a number of Lenin busts. He has deliberately placed them in open spaces on his land, in order to expose them to nature. They are occasionally modified by visiting artists and his children, who paint or damage them.
Obyrok, Chernihiv Region. 12 September 2016

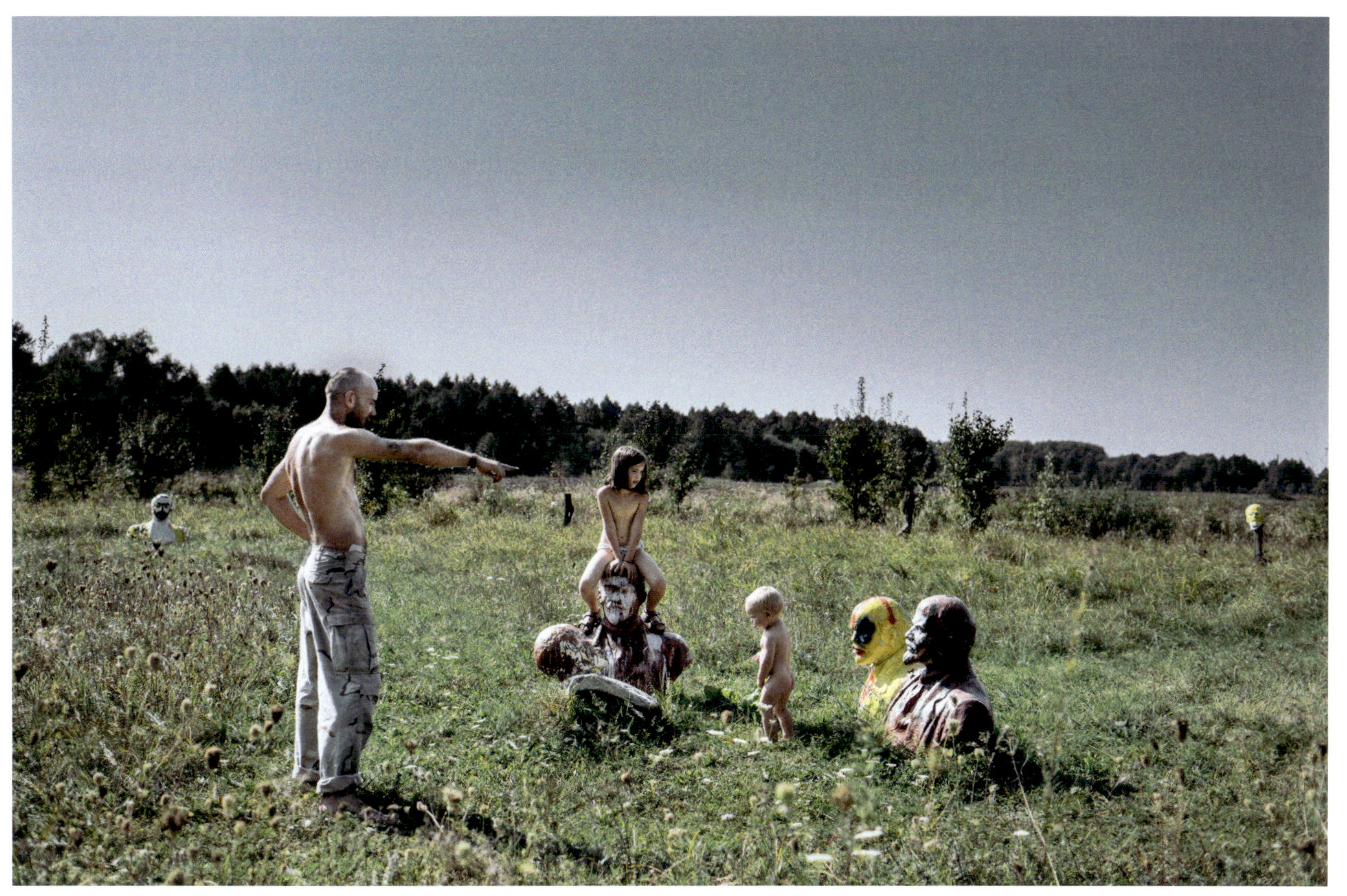

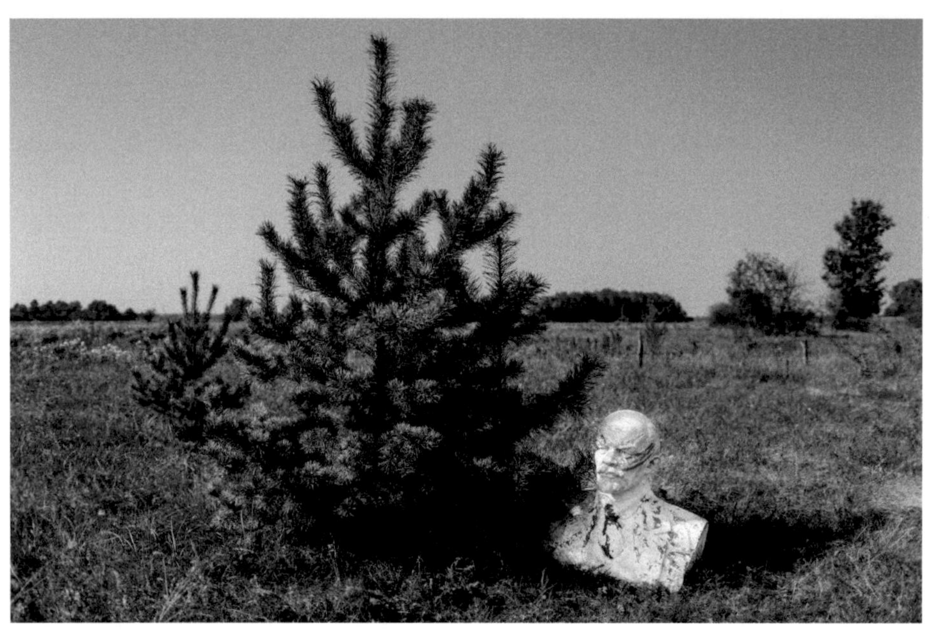

Obyrok, Chernihiv Region. 12 September 2016

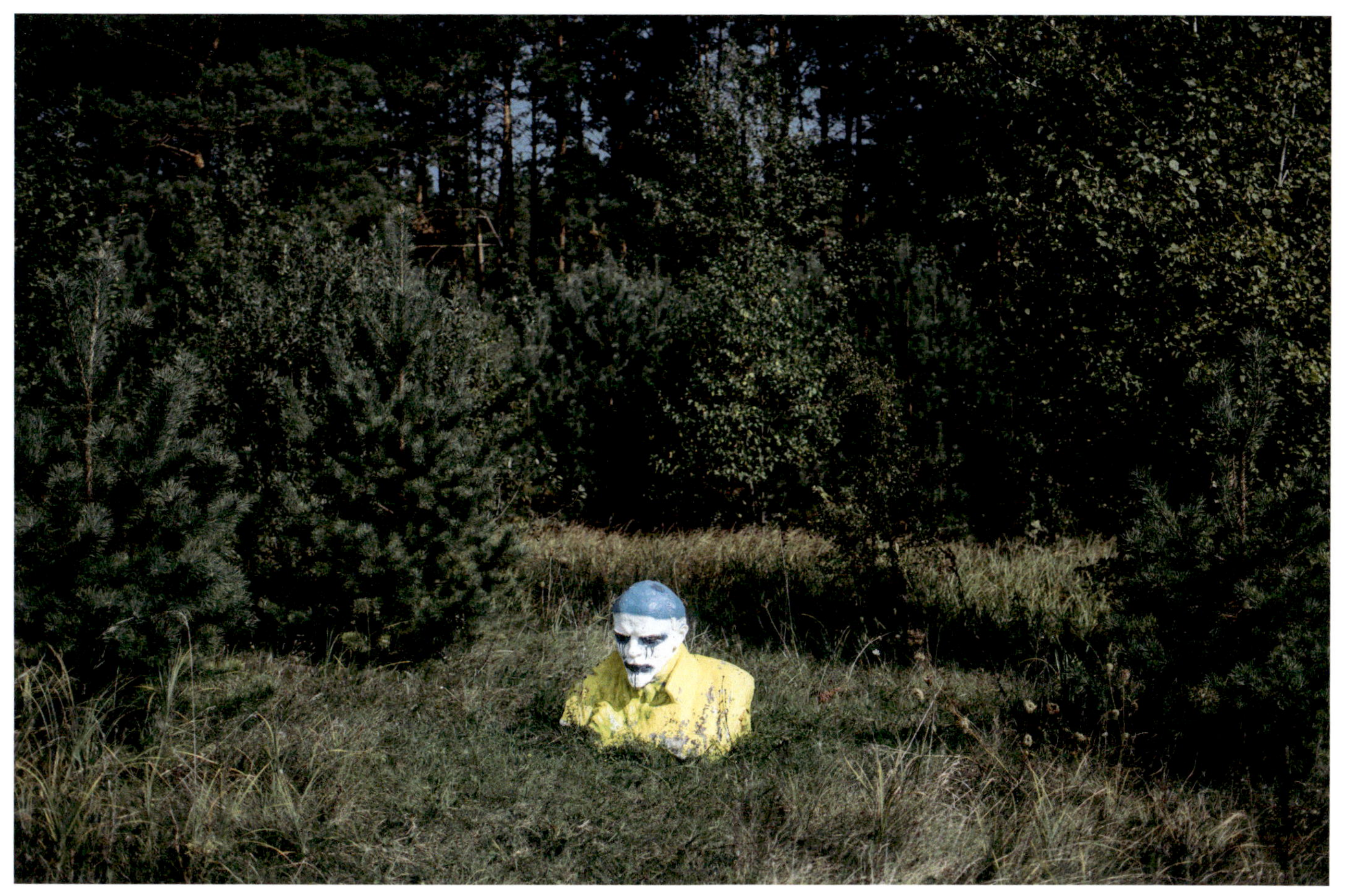

This Lenin has been transformed into a Cossack. He wears a vyshyvanka shirt, carries a bulava club and has been given a chupryna haircut. He welcomes visitors at the entrance to a leisure club on the Dnipro River. The Cossacks were a diverse group of warriors who once ruled the steppes of what is now Central and Eastern Ukraine. Their autonomy, coupled with a hostile relationship towards the Russian empire, has made them symbols of freedom and independence to modern Ukrainians.
Cherkasy. 30 March 2016

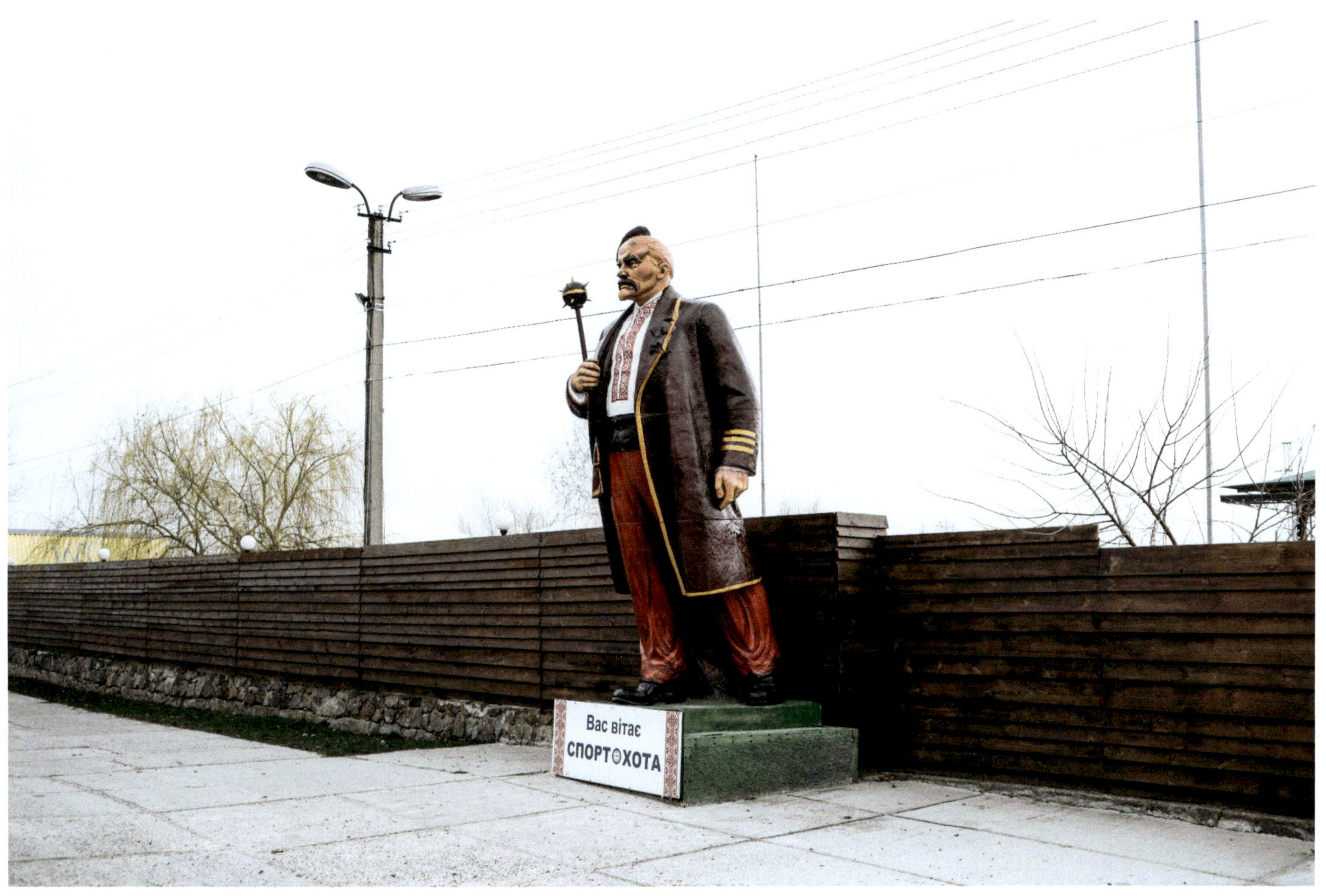

Вас вітає
СПОРТ ХОТА

The monument is stored in such a way as to protect it from damage or theft. The mayor plans to sell this
statue to foreign collectors in order to finance new projects for the city.
Hlukhiv. 12 September 2016

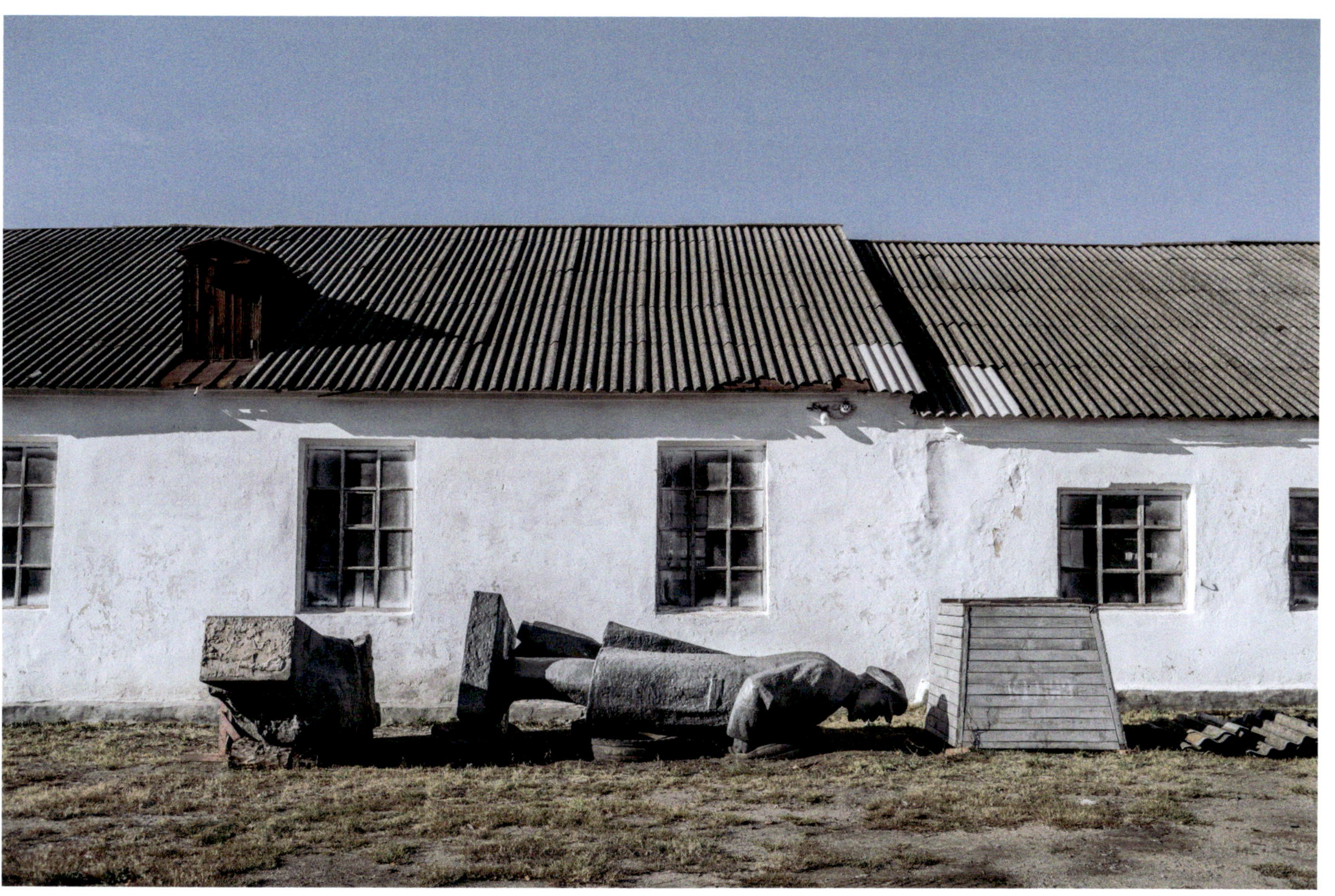

A Lenin head sits in the garden of a volunteer who assisted the Ukrainian Army in fighting against Russian-backed separatist forces in the Donbass region. It was given to her as a birthday present by a group of soldiers she had helped.
Kyiv. 30 June 2016

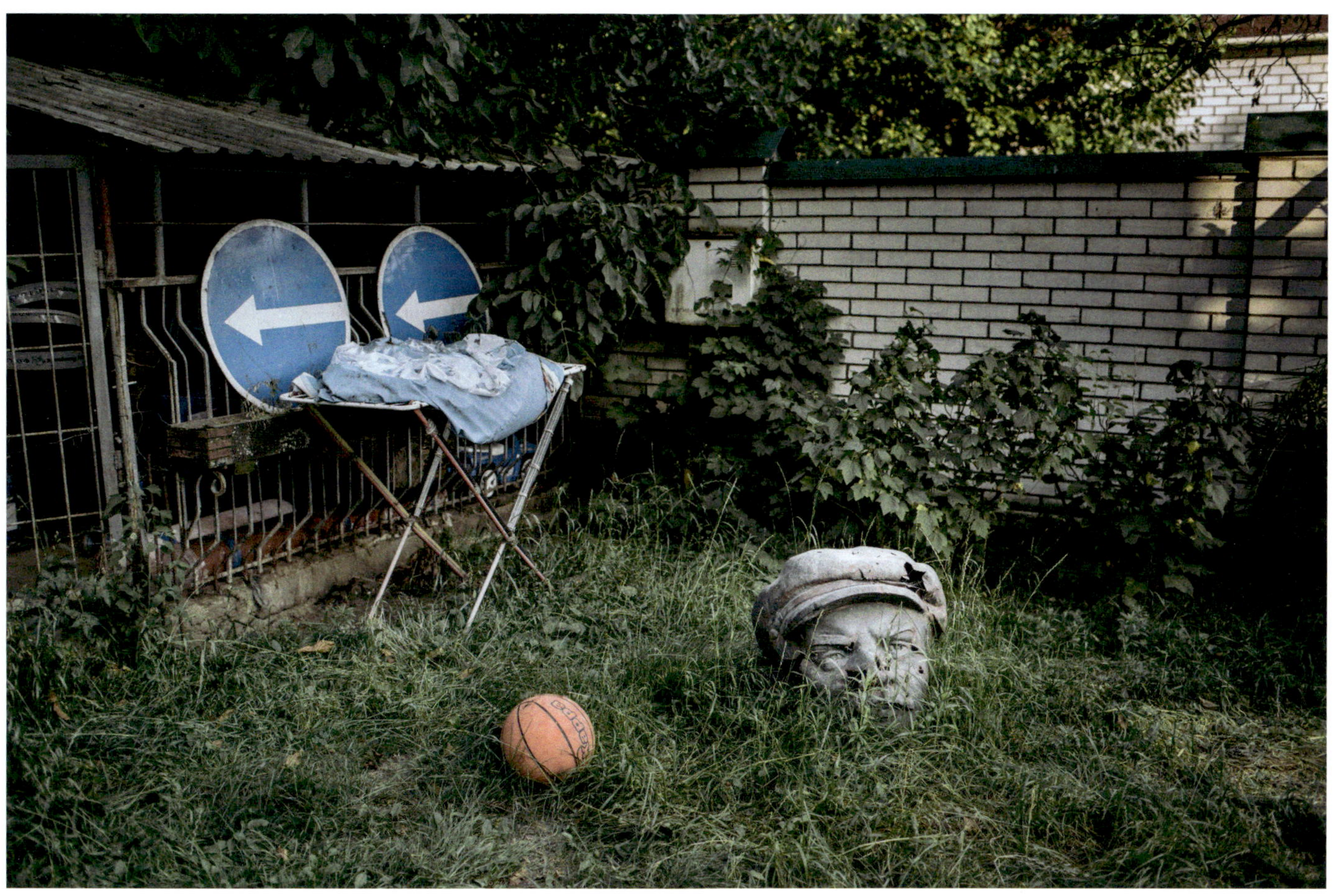

They called me and warned me they were going to take it down. I took it home because I had to, otherwise they were going to destroy it. I took it because it's important to protect these things. There is a saying: 'if you shoot at history with a gun, it will shoot back with artillery.' If everything is altered so that we forget where we come from, we will not be a nation. We will simply be people, or even worse: slaves. How many times has history been rewritten over the course of mankind? And look at the result… It all goes in circles and we make the same mistakes over and over again. Personally, I have nothing against Lenin. My family received a land plot under his New Economic Policy [1921-24]. It was only later that we lost everything because of collectivisation. My family was spared from purges and repressions because my grandfather worked with the NKVD [the forerunner of the KGB]. Lenin remained a symbol of hope. If you could see how traumatised the villagers are… For them, decommunisation is really brutal and shameless. They grew up and lived through the Soviet era. And now, people who actually went through those same times come and tell them it was all meaningless. Have some respect! You see what I mean?

Oleksandr
Shabo Village Council Representative, Shabo

He's the head of evil. And now he's in my garden… That's quite ironic. I started to travel back and forth to the frontline at the very beginning of the conflict in Donbass. To supply and support our soldiers there. And then one day, a group of them came to me and gave me this head – for my birthday… I don't even know where it's from, but you can see that it was destroyed by artillery. 'Decommunisation by military means', they told me. Then they thought it would make a nice, unique present for me, to have the head of the enemy at home… I don't really believe it's a nice present, but there was no way to refuse it… So now I'm thinking I'll wait a bit for it to gain value, then I'll organise an auction and sell it. Hopefully I'll get enough money to buy supplies for our guys on the frontline. Then Vladimir Ilyich will do some good for the world – probably for the first and last time!

Diana
Volunteer, Kyiv

There isn't a single Lenin left standing within 100 kilometres of Kryvyi Rih. We've been very active. One evening we toppled four of them! The local authorities are former Communists. They didn't want to implement the law on decommunisation. We wrote to them. We drew them maps, showing the location of every Lenin still standing. But they didn't lift a finger. So we acted on our own. Now you see, I keep the heads. I have to be discreet because there are some ongoing investigations looking for the statues. But I keep them. Not out of nostalgia. I want to sell them, so I can pay for the medical assistance for a friend of mine. He was injured while fighting in Donbass… That's what Lenin should be used for.

Yaroslav
Civic activist, Kryvyi Rih

Lenin? I don't want to talk about it. He's gone, that's it. If you want to know about him, open a history book – don't bother me, I have a lot of work to do. It's on the municipal wasteland now, we'll keep it until we manage to sell it. It's metal, so I can get a bit of money for the city budget. We really need the money. People need to think about something else, that's it. We've decommunised everything in Hlukhiv. The main street was named after Lenin, the citizens decided to rename it. Now it's called Tereshenko, after my family. I had nothing to do with it. I don't see myself as a new idol who came to save them. The people chose the new name…

Michel Tereshchenko
Mayor, Hlukhiv

The nationalist group Sokil claim that all the monuments of Lenin within a 100-kilometre radius of Kryvyi Rih have been removed. They want to sell these 'trophies' to pay for the medical care of their friend who was injured while fighting against Russian-backed separatists in Donbass.
Kryvyi Rih. 8 June 2016

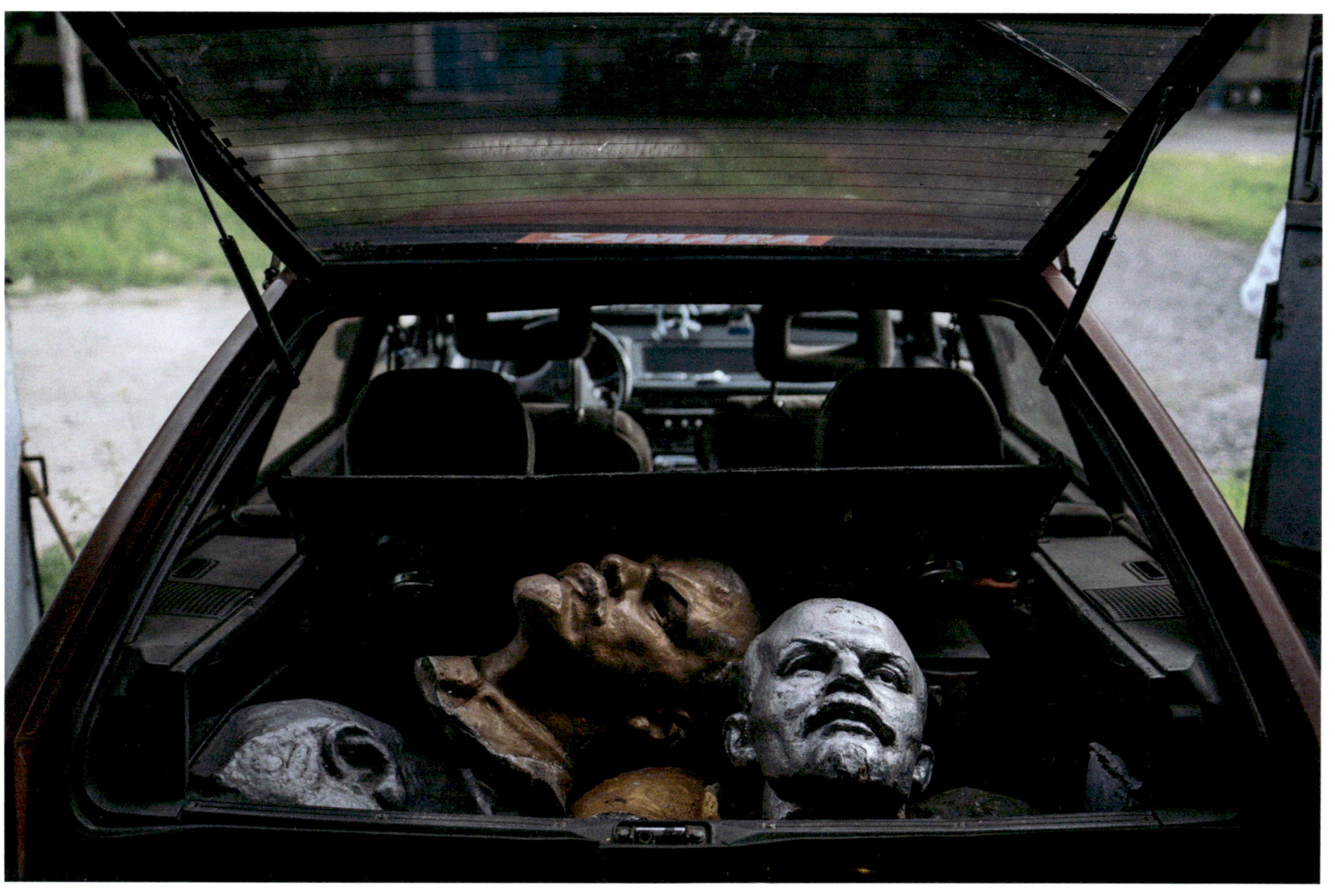

The melted-down leg of the local Lenin monument was used to make this statue entitled *The Olympian* in honour of four-time Olympic champion Volodymyr Holubnychyi. Unfortunately, Holubnychyi himself has confirmed that it does not resemble him.
Sumy. 13 September 2016

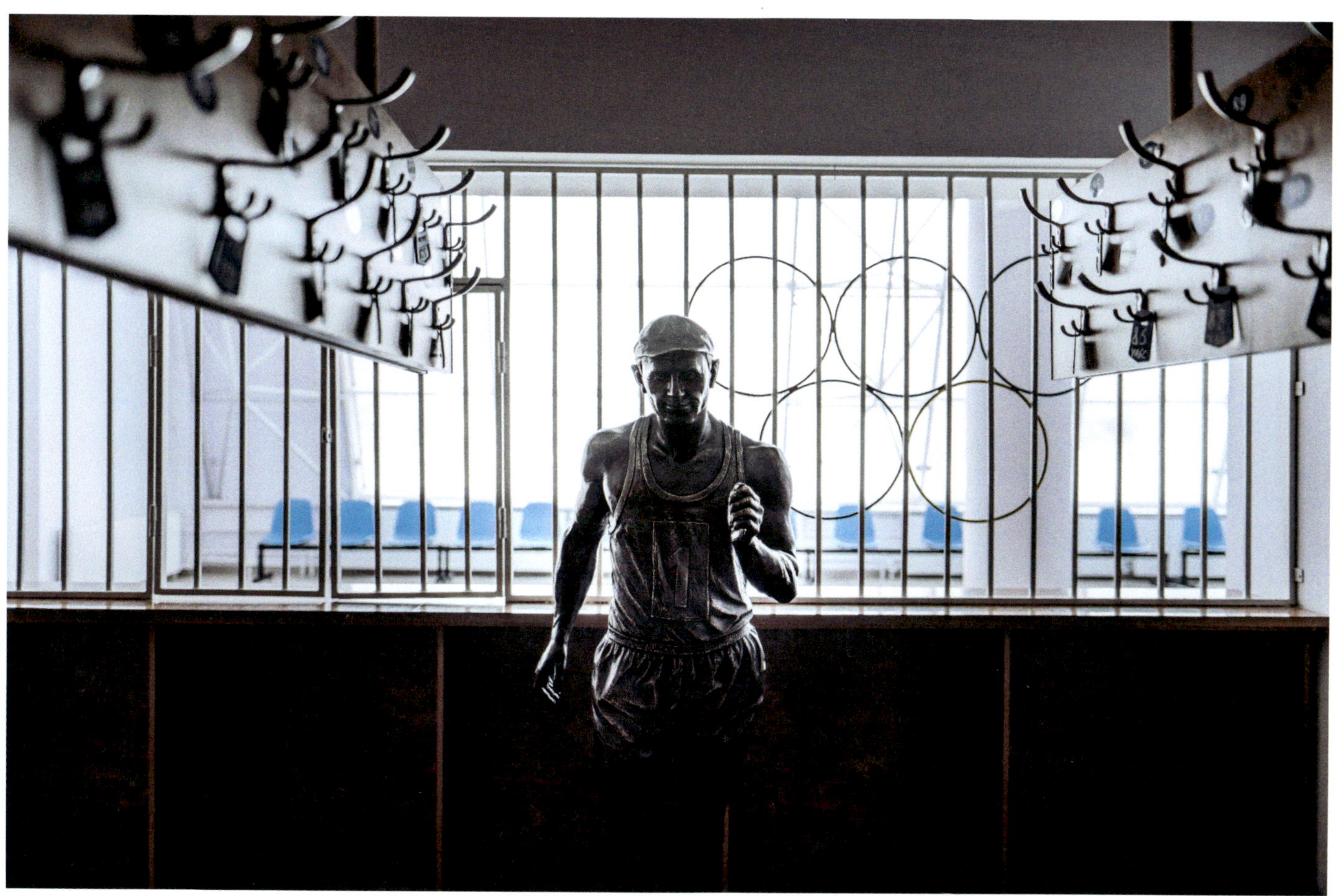

Shabo, Odessa Region. 21 November 2015

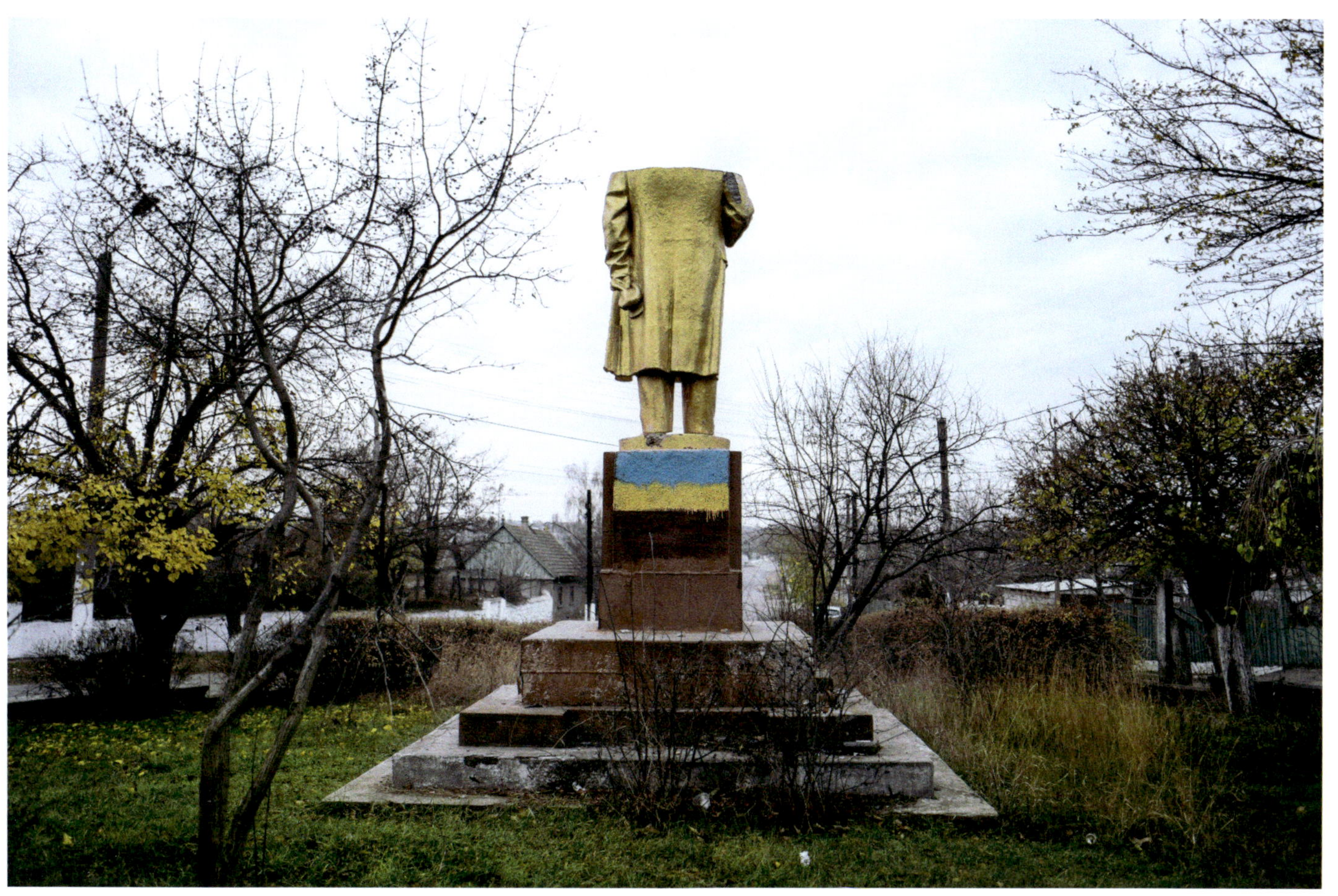

The head of the beheaded monument photographed the year before in the same village (see previous page).
Shabo, Odessa Region. 2 October 2016

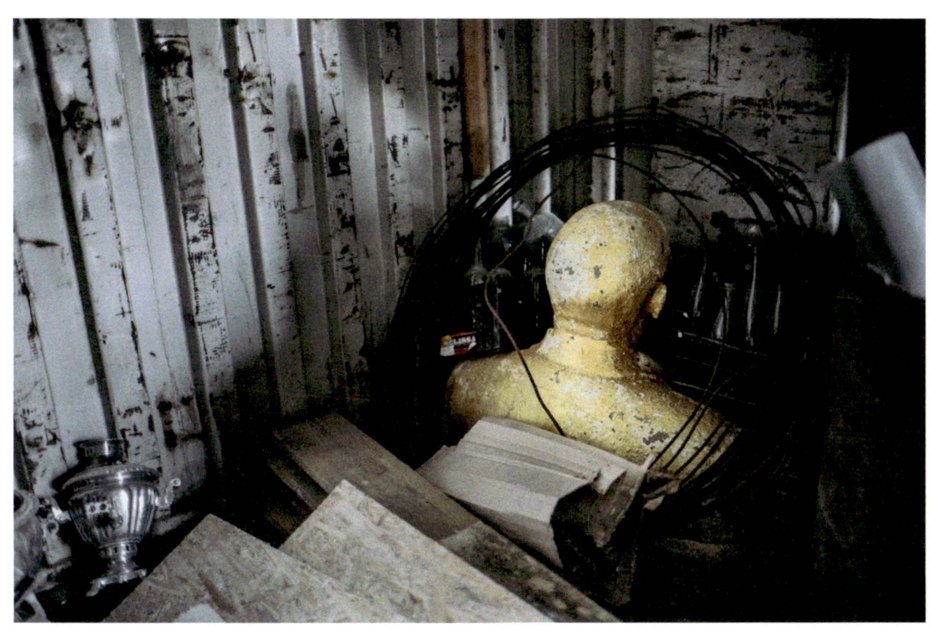

The village of Korzhi is attempting to sell its statue for 15000 dollars to fund repairs to the local kindergarten and school. The price is high and there have been no offers. The local mechanic in charge of the sale expects he will eventually have to trade it for scrap metal for less than 3000 dollars.
Korzhi. 3 June 2016

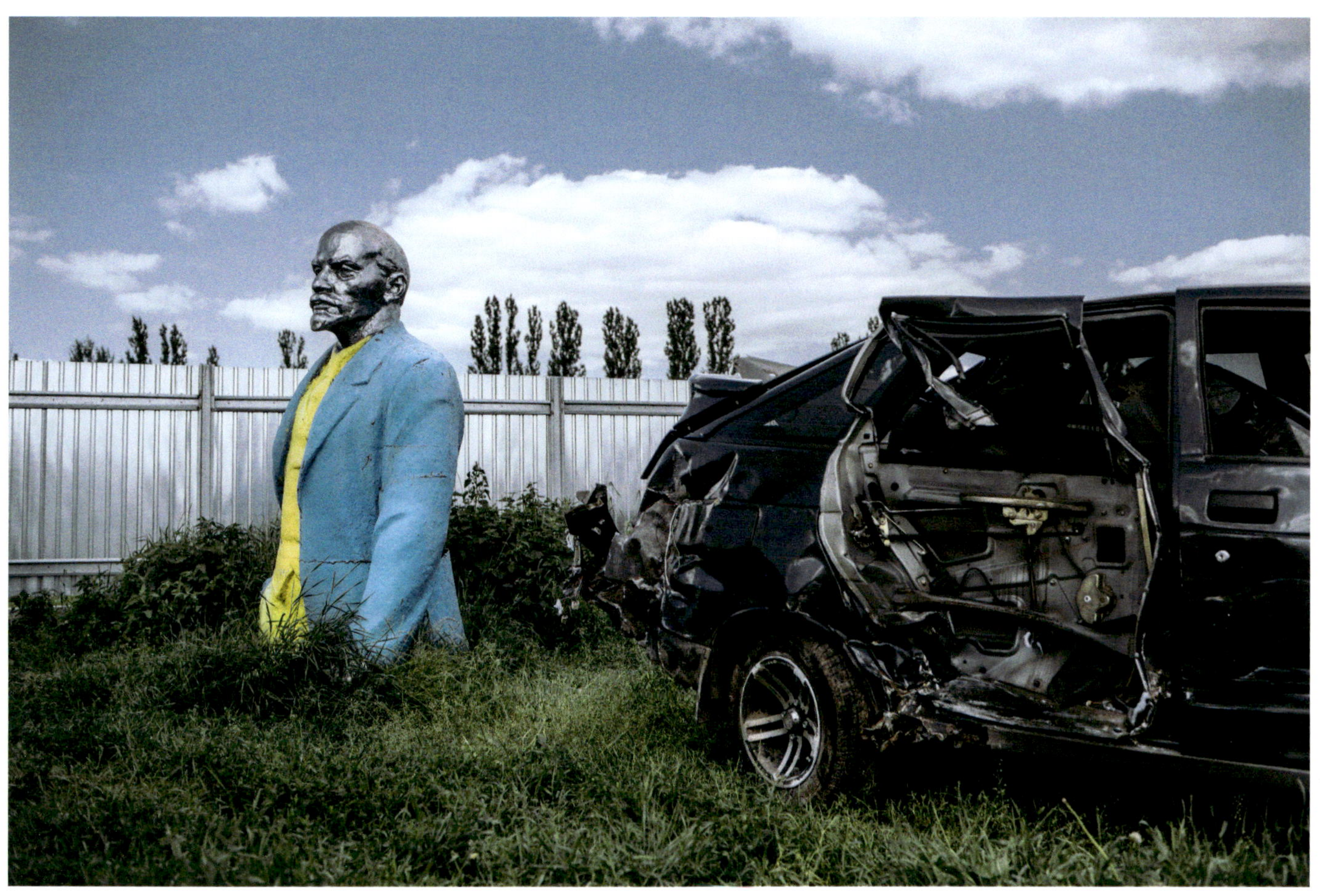

Kramatorsk. 17 September 2015

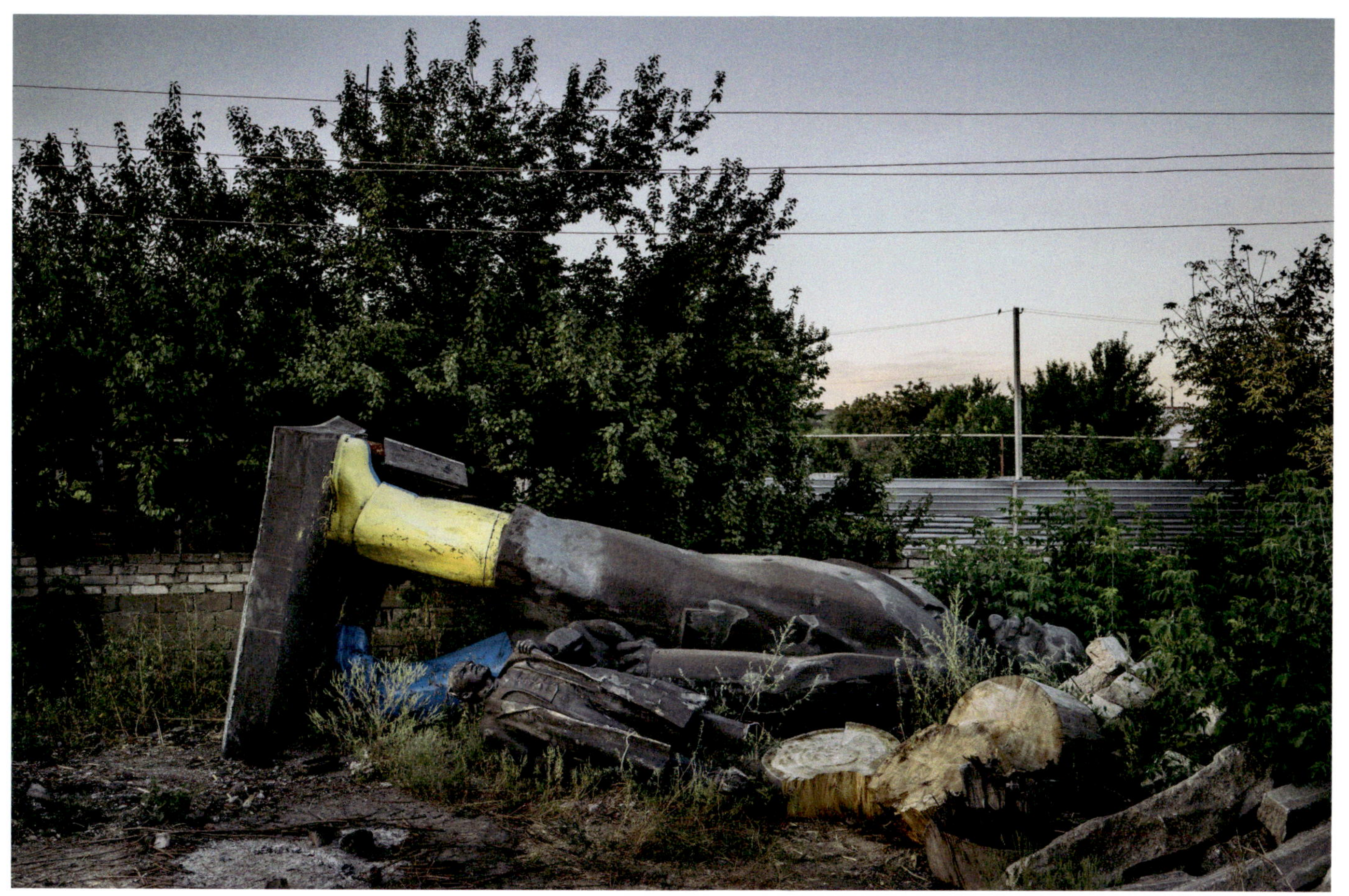

Podobovets, Carpathian Mountains. 2 November 2016

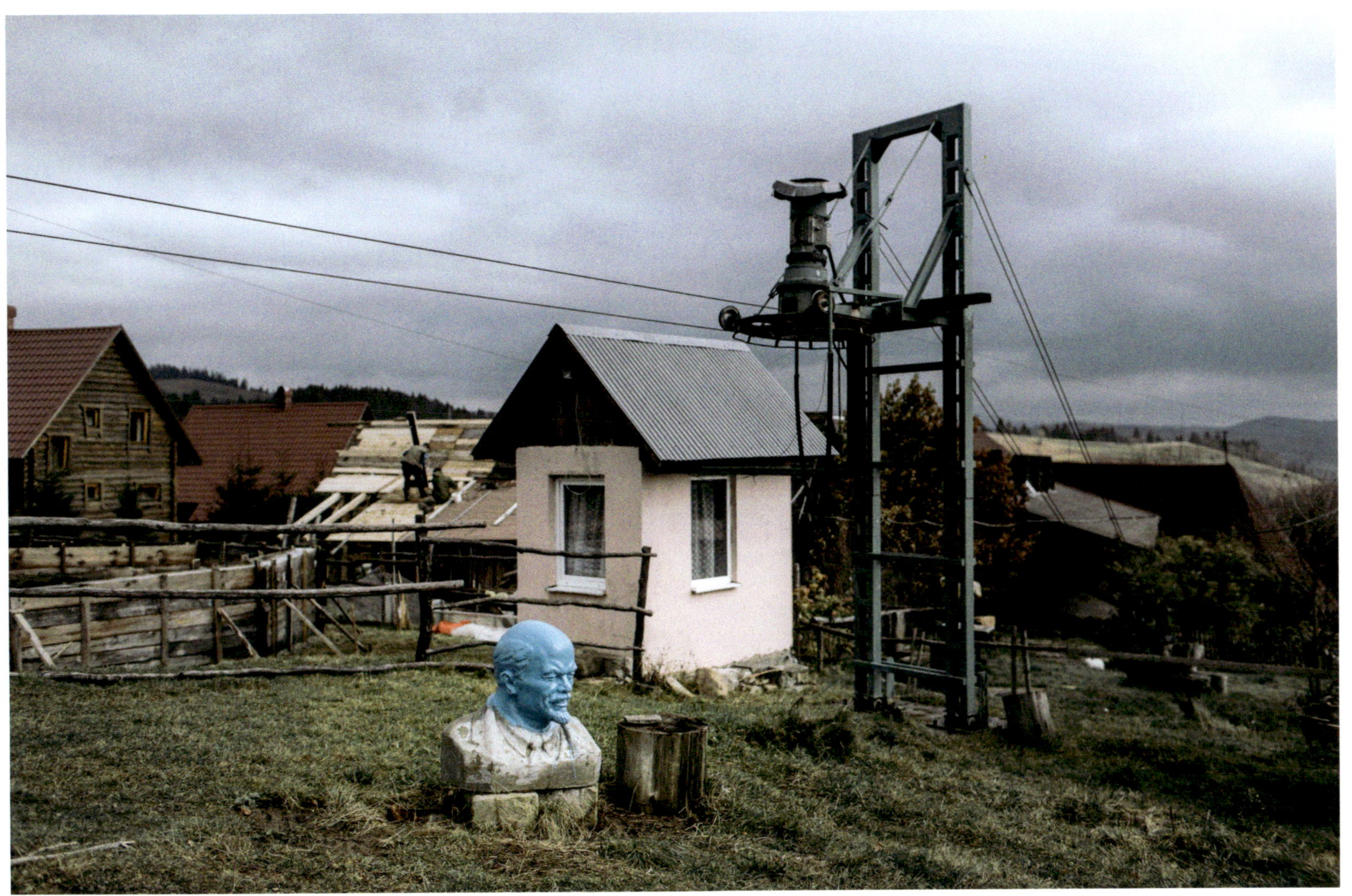

When we had to make a decision about this huge Lenin on Freedom Square, it wasn't a question of whether to decommunise or not. Remember that in Kharkiv, it was a matter of war or peace. War or peace. Back then, we were all mobilised to defend our city. They say I was the head of the movement. But it wasn't that noble. There came a point where no one had grabbed the megaphone – so I had to do it. I started to scream and encourage the guys. It doesn't make me the leader of anything. Nor does it make us champions of decommunisation for that matter… We observed tendencies: the places where Lenin was still standing were the areas of unrest and separatist agitation. It was probably connected to the idea of the 'Russian world' or something like that. So it meant that to protect our city, we had to topple Lenin, to mark our city as Ukrainian territory. I remember that in our group, we felt that nothing was impossible. You know, we were those sort of young and over-motivated people. 'One for all, and all for one!', if you remember The Three Musketeers. So it was also a challenge for us, to take down Lenin, because no one believed it was possible. It seemed as if the statue was rooted in the square. And we did it. I really grew as a man during the time I defended the city. Yet I realise now that it was only the beginning.

Valentyn Bystrychenko
Civil activist, Kharkiv

You are looking for Lenin? Good for you. I'll help you but let's move fast: I have a lot of work to do. I don't really care about decommunisation. Neither do the city residents. In Chernihiv, there are few economic opportunities, we don't have many jobs to offer. Our city is neglected. We need to develop businesses and attract investments and provide a future for our kids – that's our priority. They took Lenin away. Good. But this didn't change anything in our lives.

Oleksandr Lomako
Deputy mayor, Chernihiv

Sure, I know about Lenin: I was one of those who took down the statue on Bessarabska Square [Kyiv] in December 2014! My family are all from Western Ukraine. We used to be quite wealthy before the Soviets came, but they took everything. Several members of my family fought in the UPA [the Ukrainian Insurgent Army] in the 1940s it goes without saying that we were never big fans of Lenin. So I helped to take it down, it was a pleasure. Did I keep a piece of it? Are you joking? Anything connected to Lenin is evil!

Yurko Dosiak
Former volunteer, Donbass Battalion, Lviv

He's been here for several winters now, on the ground, facing the mountains. Kids play with him, they turn him into a snowman, we put a funny hat on him… I don't know where he comes from. I don't know how the landlady got her hands on him. I don't even know why they painted him blue. I do know that I've been telling the landlady to move it away from her property. It brings bad vibrations and misfortune. She doesn't have to take it too far away. Just 50 metres. Off her property, at least. Plus there are neighbours around, we have to think about their well-being! But the landlady doesn't listen to me. She says she wants to create some kind of landmark for tourists. They travel to the Carpathian Mountains and… Surprise! There is old Vova [the familiar form of the name Vladimir]. But lots of tourists don't understand it. I don't understand it, that's for sure. I don't know what it's doing here.

Yuri
Assistant to the landlady, Podobovets

Look, it's in here! My God, they cut it apart, it's all in pieces. I remember I used to play around this statue when I was a little girl. It stood on the main square, just like everywhere else. Wow, look at his boot! How much do you think it weighs? 200 kilos? I remember the statue was really huge… Now, it looks so small. I'm not interested in it personally, my editor just asked me to look for it to produce a report for the two-year anniversary of its dismantlement. Do you know that a guy stole the pieces for a few weeks? When the police arrested him, he claimed he wanted to sell them for 'patriotic purposes' — crazy people! Two years ago, that's all it was. Now it's here, in a wooden house at the back of the cemetery, cut into pieces.

Alina Korzhynska
Journalist, Chernihiv

Rivne's Lenin monument was toppled on 25 August 1991 – a day after the Verkhovna Rada (the Supreme Council of Ukraine) declared independence. It was then cut into pieces and transported to Lviv. Here the metal was melted down and reworked into a statue of Ukrainian poet Taras Shevchenko.
Rivne. 21 November 2016

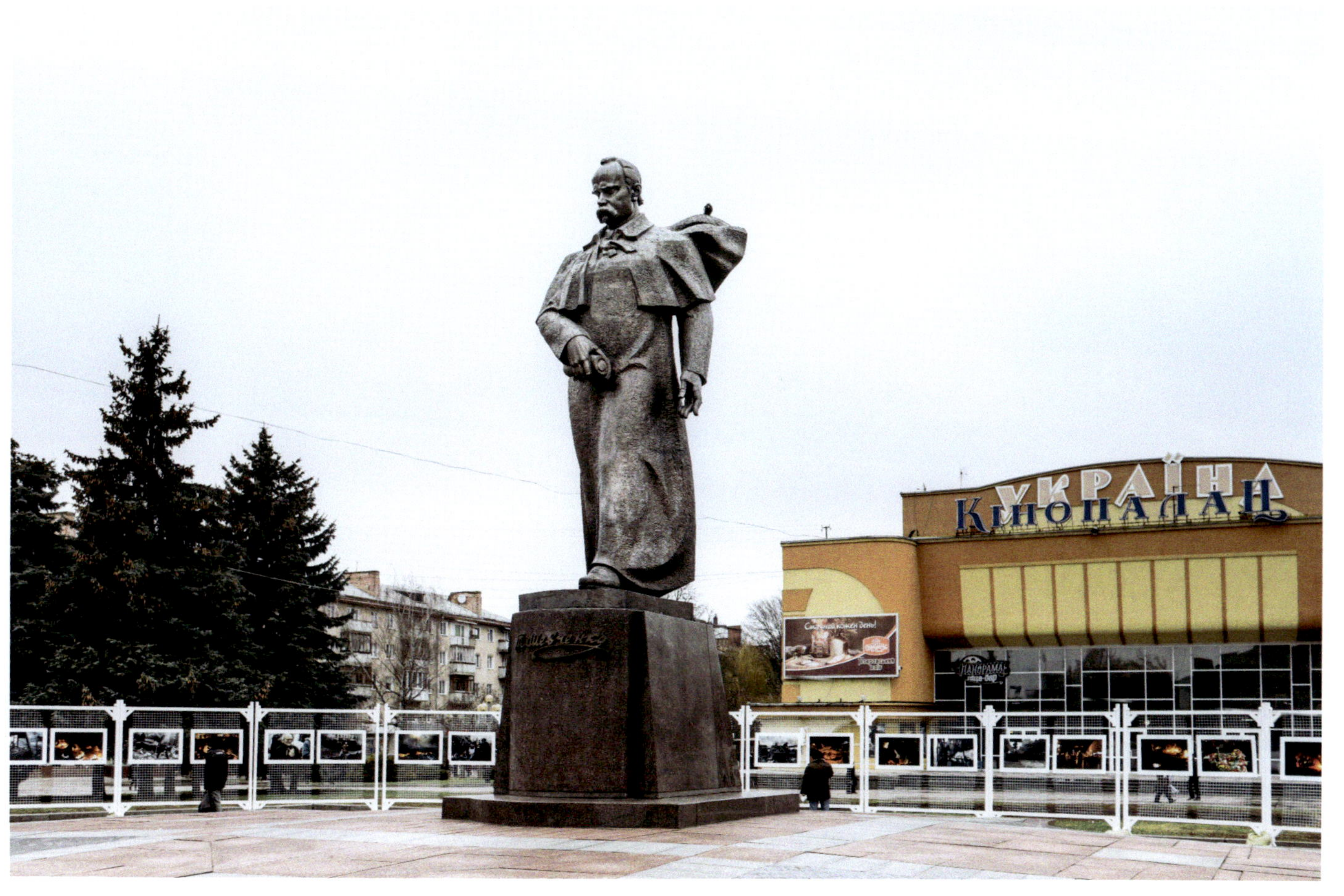

УКРАЇНА
КІНОПАЛАЦ

Ukrainian artist Oleksandr Milov has transformed this Lenin statue into the *Star Wars* character Darth
Vader. It stands in a factory courtyard on the outskirts of Odessa.
Odessa. 21 November 2015

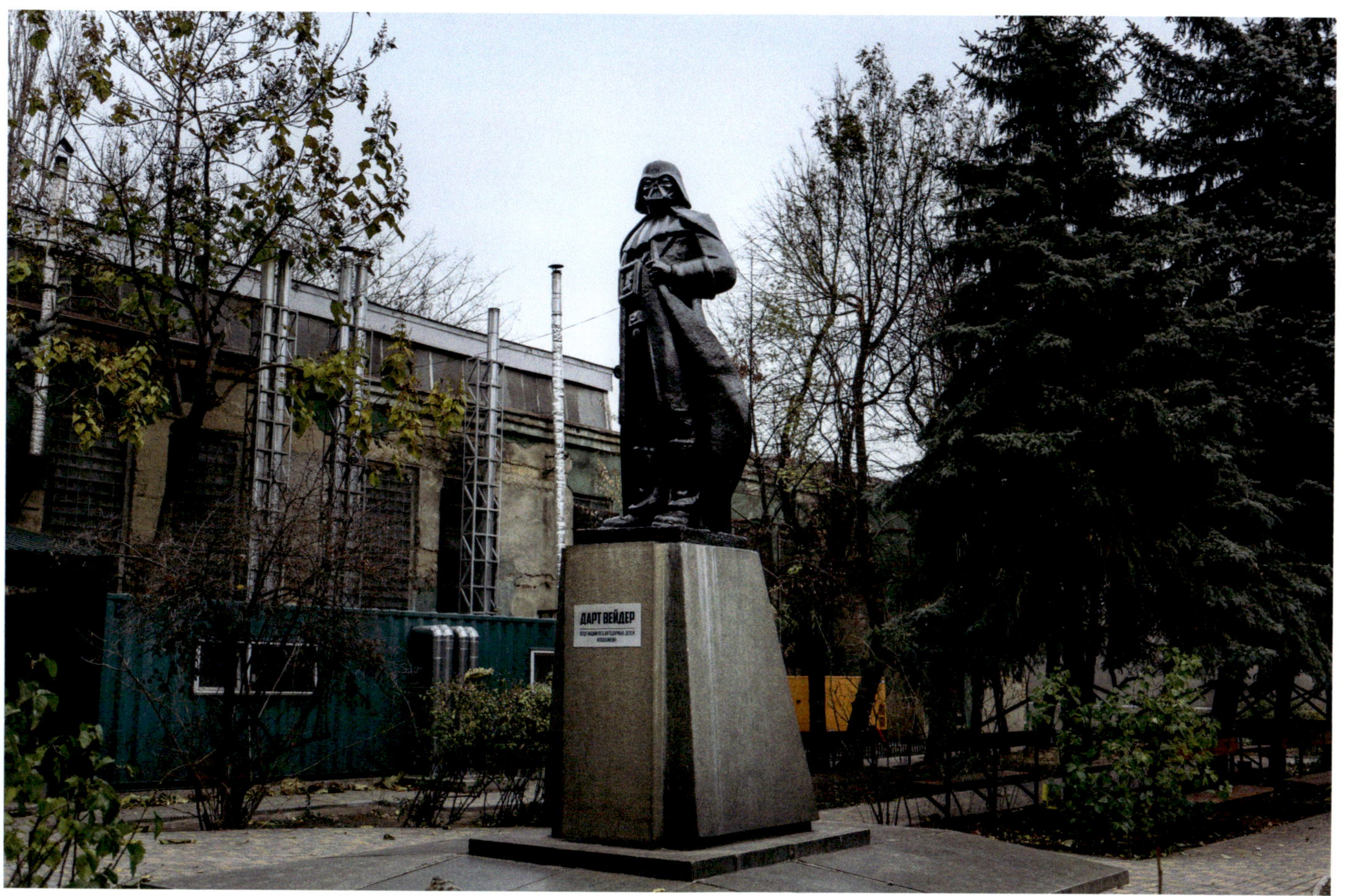

ДАРТ ВЕЙДЕР

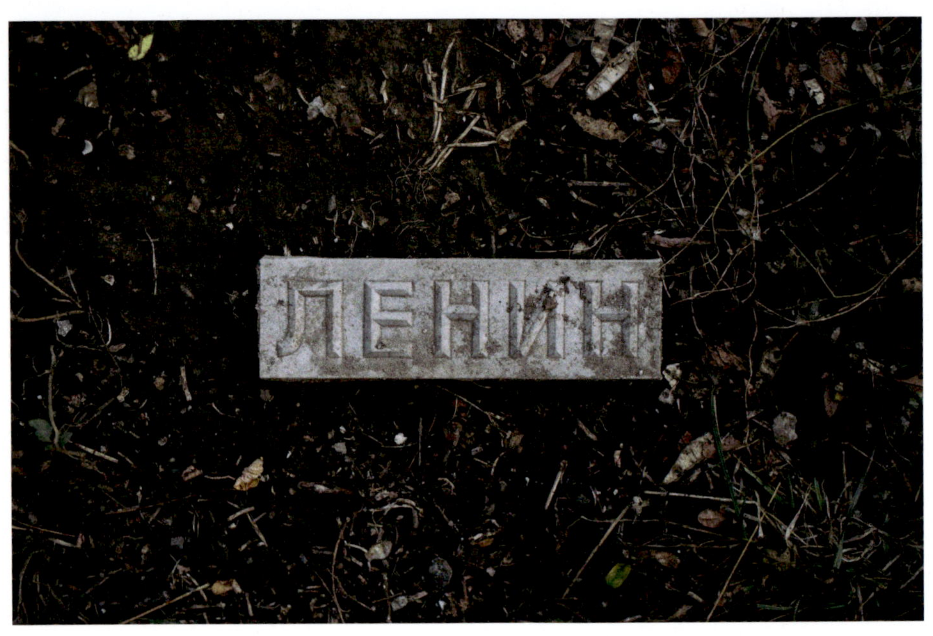

'Dyadya Kolya' (Uncle Nikolai) protects his bust of Lenin. Nationalists have attempted to steal it on three seperate occaisions and have even tried to bury it.
Berdyansk. 30 September 2016

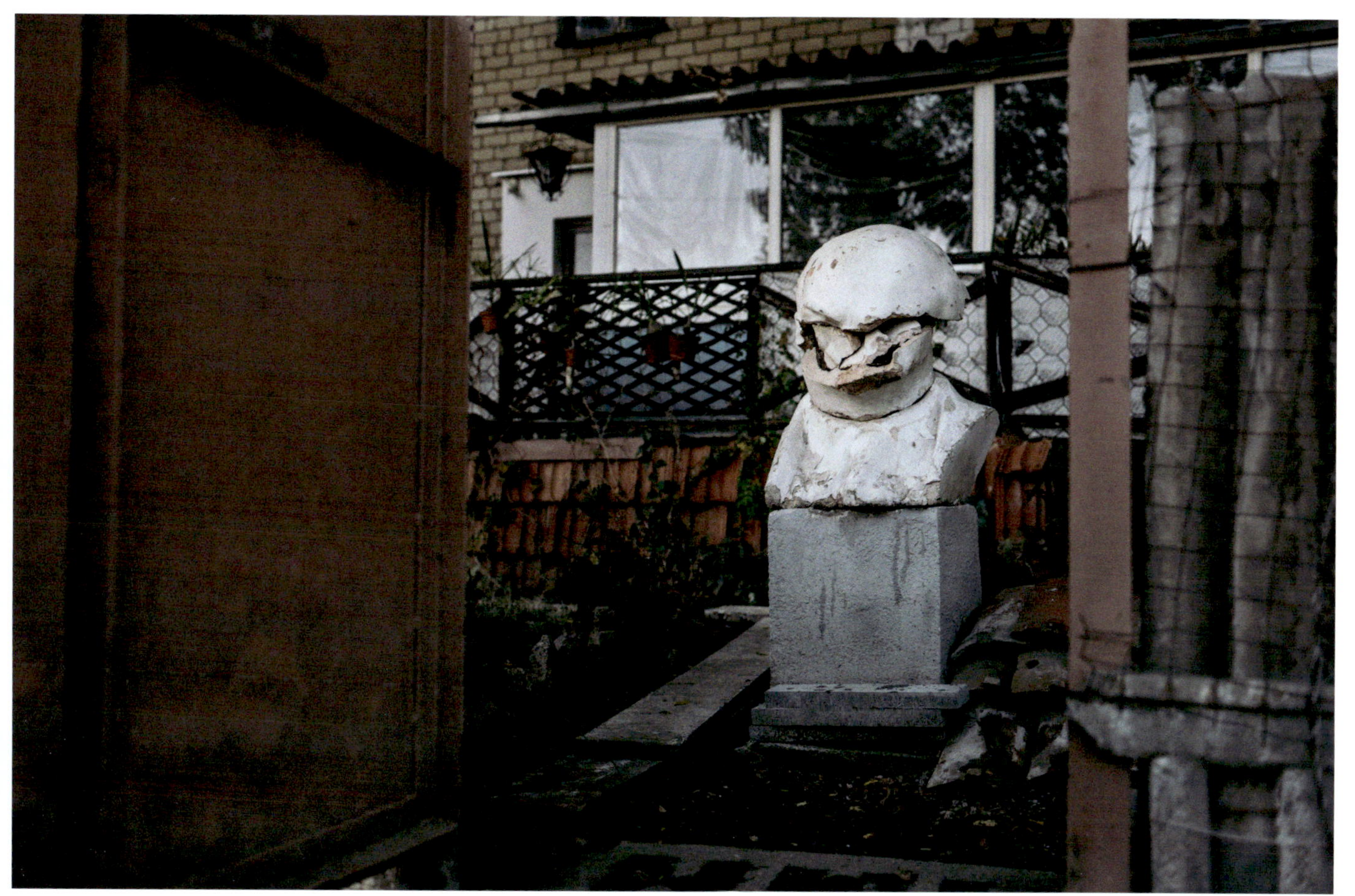

Teplivka. 26 July 2016

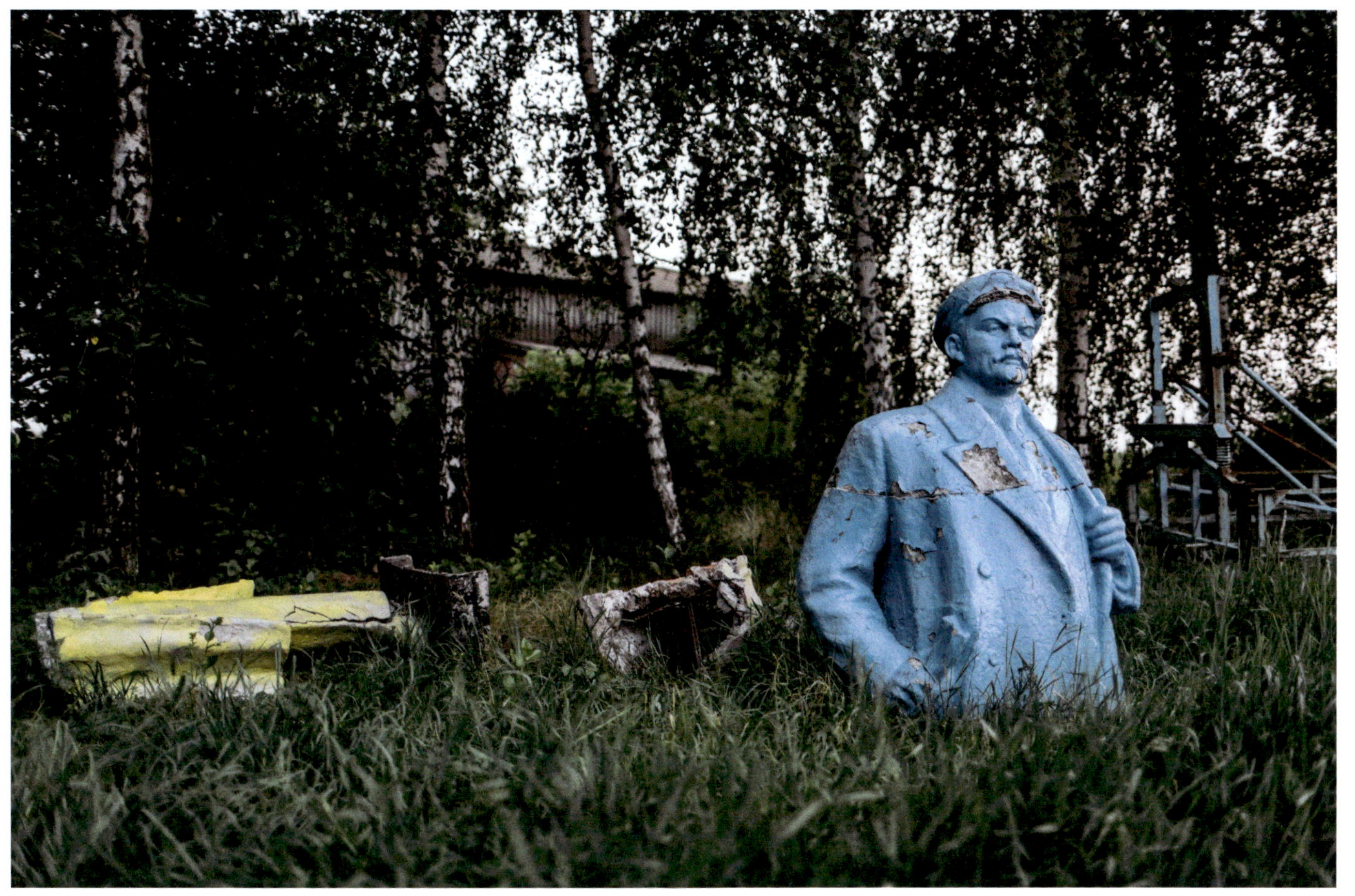

Volnovakha. 1 October 2016

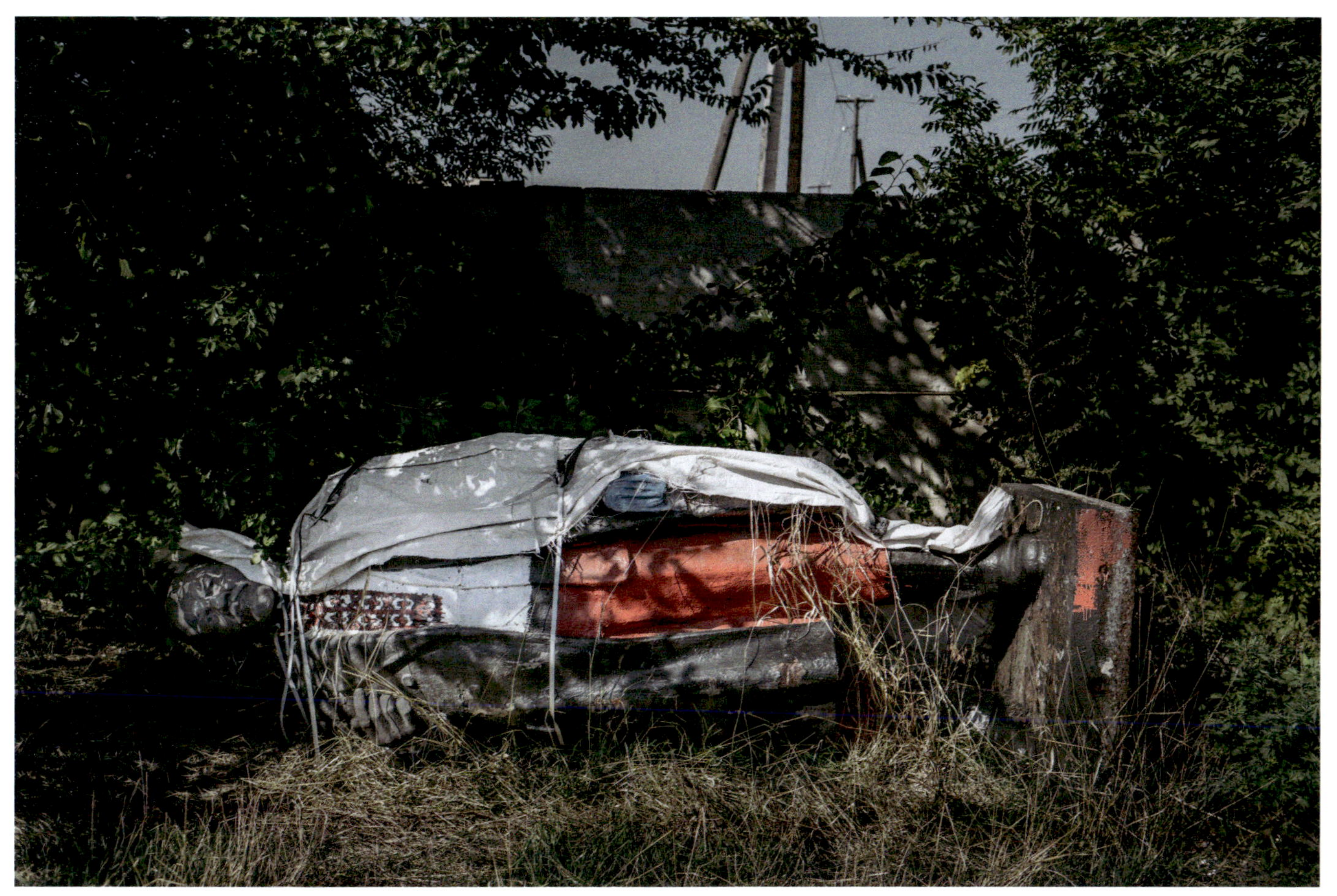

Chernihiv's Lenin was seized and cut into pieces by local activist Oleksiy Korzh. He intended to sell the metal to finance a new work of art for the city. But the monument belongs to the city administration, so the police were called to recover it. After weighing the pieces, it became apparent that 1 tonne of the original 3.5-tonne statue is missing.
Chernihiv. 6 May 2016

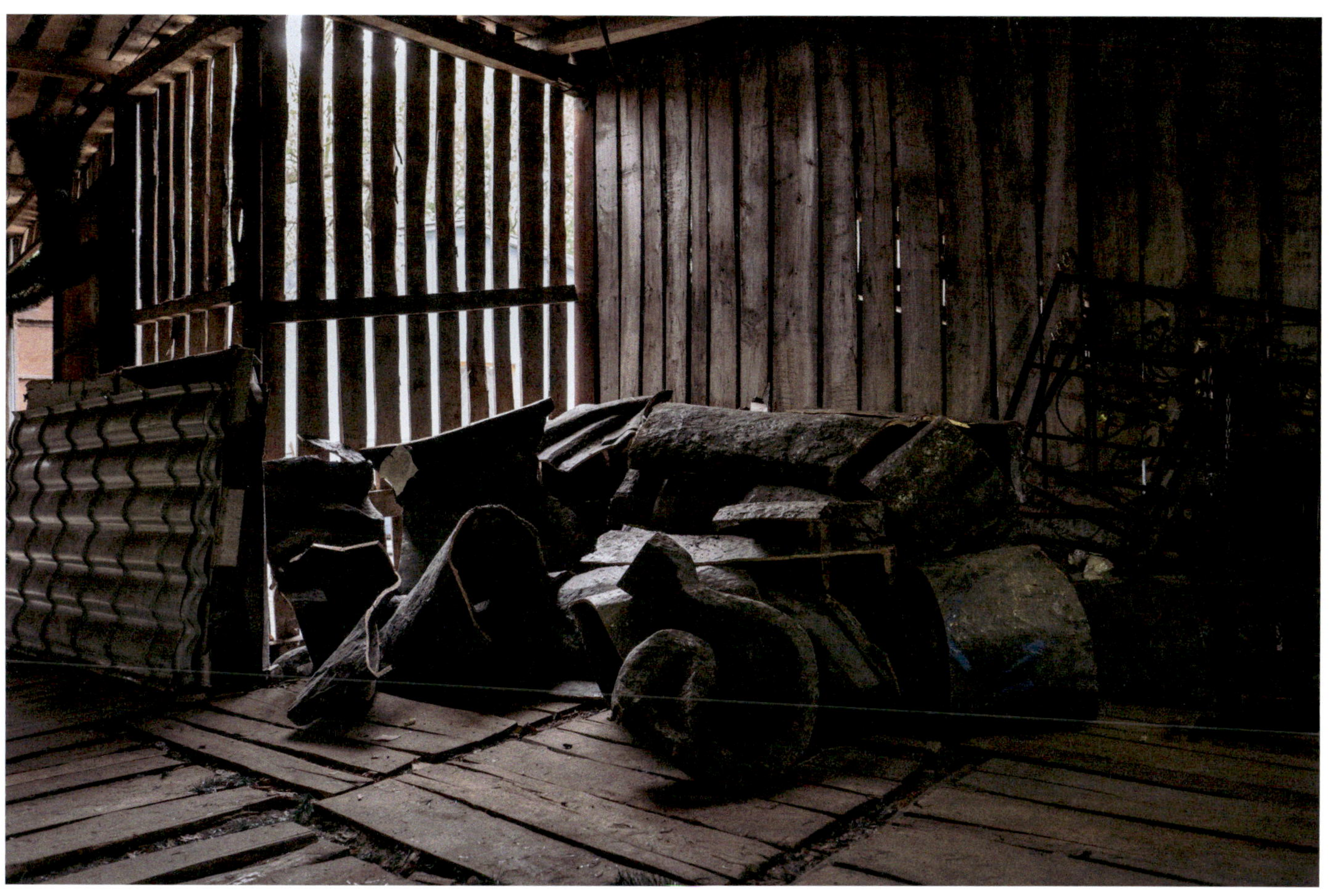

This nose belonged to the Kharkiv statue of Lenin, which at 8.5 metres was once the largest in Ukraine.
When this picture was taken, it was on display at the Pinchuk Art Centre in Kyiv as part of Yevgenia
Belorusets's installation *Let's Put Lenin's Head Back Together Again!* (2015).
Kyiv. 5 February 2016

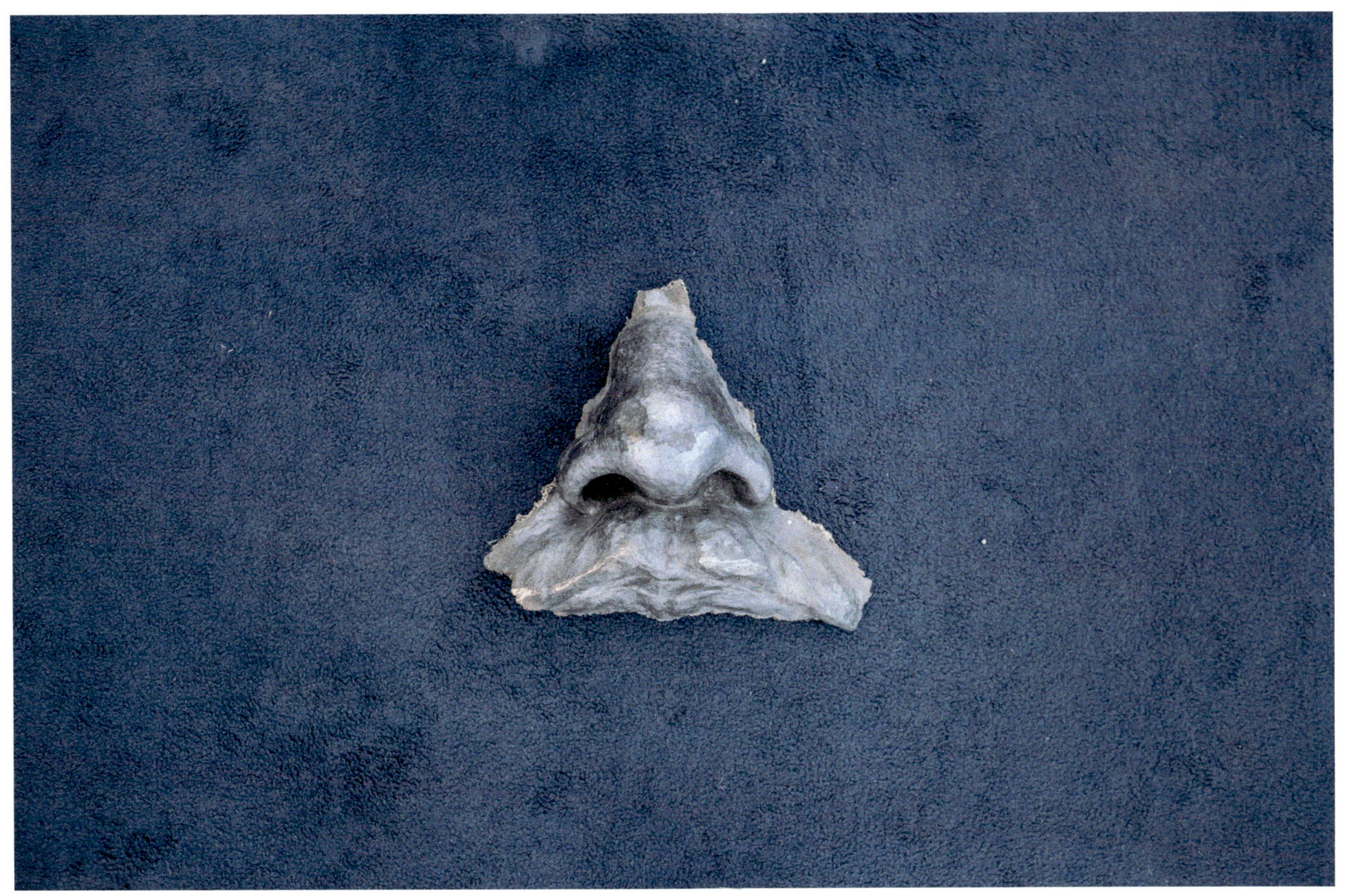

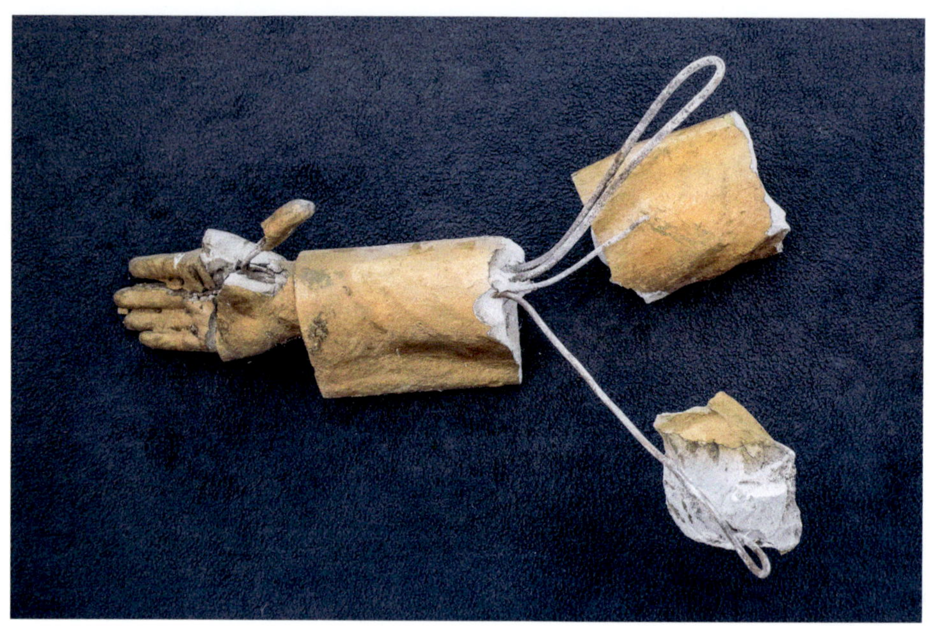

These Lenin fragments belong to monuments from unknown locations in Ukraine. They also form part of
Yevgenia Belorusets's installation titled, *Let's Put Lenin's Head Back Together Again!* (see previous page).
Kyiv. 5 February 2016

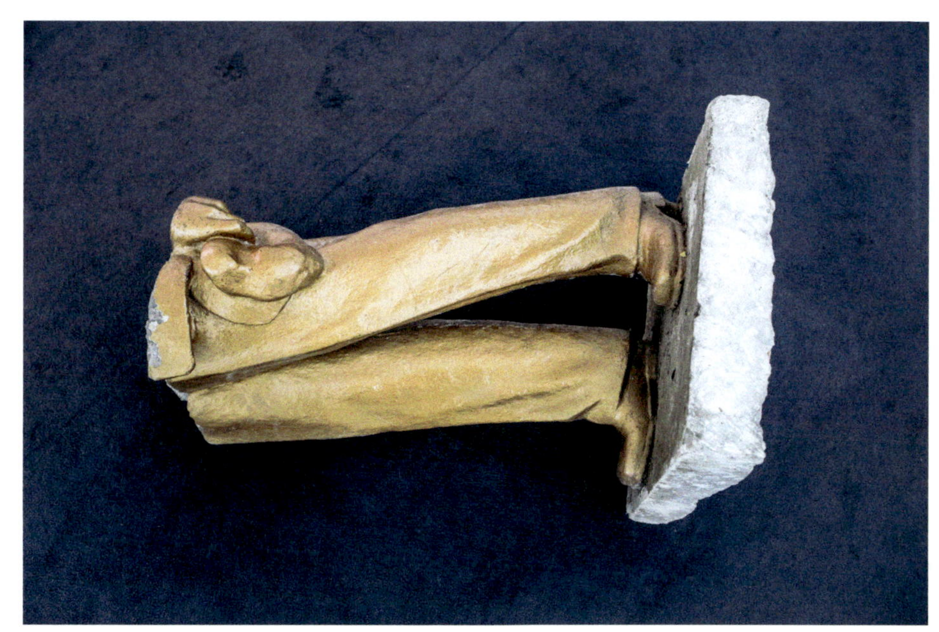

The owner of the farm, she's an old lady. One day she ordered us to raise the Lenin statue that was lying in the courtyard. She said she wanted Dyadya Vova [Uncle Vlad] to stand, so he could contemplate the state of Ukraine today.

Security guard
Tsybuleve

It is important to differentiate between Lenin and other Soviet objects and works of art. Lenin is the symbol of the former regime, and of everything wrong that came with it. He is the sacrifice we make on the altar of decommunisation, to turn the page, so to speak. Other objects, such as paintings, mosaics, sculptures or buildings, don't carry such an ideological charge. At least, we have to agree that they have gradually lost their ideological meaning over the past twenty-five years. For most people, they're works of art. Yet the current process of decommunisation does not establish such a difference. National authorities — in particular the Ukrainian Institute of National Remembrance, under the directorship of Volodymyr Viatrovych — claim there is a social demand for decommunisation and use this as a pretext to get rid of anything they don't like. In doing so, they contradict the law on the preservation of national heritage. Also, in their monopolisation of the media discourse, they go against freedom of speech. They try to create a state ideology that condemns any form of criticism. This is risky because decommunisation is hard on all of us, as everyone has to redefine at least some part of their own identity. Cities in the East of the country, such as Severodonetsk or Lysychansk, are extreme examples of this. They were created through Soviet industrialism, so getting rid of their Communist past leaves them with practically no points of reference. This is very difficult. We see some frustrated and angry reactions emerging as a result. They restore ideological meaning to objects that lost it a long time ago. We then witness a form of renaissance for these mosaics, paintings, sculptures and so on, as they regain their original ideological charge. In my opinion, nothing did more for the popularity of Soviet symbolism than the current process of decommunisation.

Yevgenia Moliar
Curator of Art Projects, Izolyatsia Foundation, Kyiv

Sit down guys! Let's have some champagne! Some home-made salo [cured slabs of fatback], apricots from my garden and homemade honey. I'll tell you everything about Lenin. In fact, I don't really know what to tell you about him, it's all very simple. He is gone — that's it. But I do know that we need to feel relaxed to talk about these things. So sit down! Drink! Eat!

Pavlo Grigorovych Prokofiev
Head of the Village Council, Oleksandrivka

It was a shock. I just unlocked the warehouse and turned on the light. He was here — massive — and staring straight at me! So I took a picture and posted it online. It turned out that no one knew he was here! Even though this is the Lenin that used to stand in front of the nuclear power plant. It's very big! Look at him. He's all stern, with a few black spots on the metal. It looks like he is contaminated with radioactivity… I would like to believe that some employee had him stored here, just in case the Soviets would come back. You know, like in the Soviet film *Wedding in Malinovka*. The villagers are so used to changes in power that they have several caps in stock, so they can swap them when some new chief comes in. Even here in Chernobyl, people think about that.

'Maksim'
Employee, Chernobyl Nuclear Power Plant

To be honest, I don't really understand what is happening — and I'm a representative of Kyiv's urban planning committee! So you can imagine what kind of a mess we're going through. Of course, when it comes to decommunisation, everything connected to the worst elements of the totalitarian past should go, that's obvious. The monument to the Cheka, the statues of Dzerzhinsky, etc. But, it's not good to destroy every Soviet monument! Some mosaics, some paintings — some Lenins even — may be considered as works of art and valued as such. At the city administration, they don't care. They receive a list of monuments to remove; they obey, without thinking. The new city council under Vitali Klitschko tries to open debates and involve citizens. At least, pretend to. I spend countless hours in public meetings, trying to explain our position and hear people out. We draw conclusions and write reports. Yet the city administration does not take into account any of our conclusions. In my opinion, they implement decommunisation with Communist methods. Which leads me to believe that our mentalities and practices won't change anytime soon. Did you see what they did in the Kyiv metro? They scratched the hammers and sickles off the walls so you can still see their shape! It's useless… and ugly. The same happens with the Lenin monuments. Someone overheard the idea that it would be good to create a park showcasing our Lenins. To attract tourists and make them pay for it. Why not? So we work on identifying a few possible sites in the city, which would be accessible for tourists and interesting to visit. We try to imagine the concept behind it. Then, one day, I receive a decision notification: it will be in a tiny strip of grass, in the middle of an industrial zone in the north of the city. That's it. They can take down as many Lenins as they want, but old habits die hard.

Anna Bondar
Deputy head, Department of Construction and Architecture, Kyiv

This Lenin head is more than 2 metres tall and previously stood on the site of the V.I. Lenin Nuclear Power Station (Chernobyl Nuclear Power Plant). It is now stored in a room used by the facility cleaning staff. Despite the authorities' claims of contamination, no significant levels of radiation were found. Chernobyl. 6 October 2016

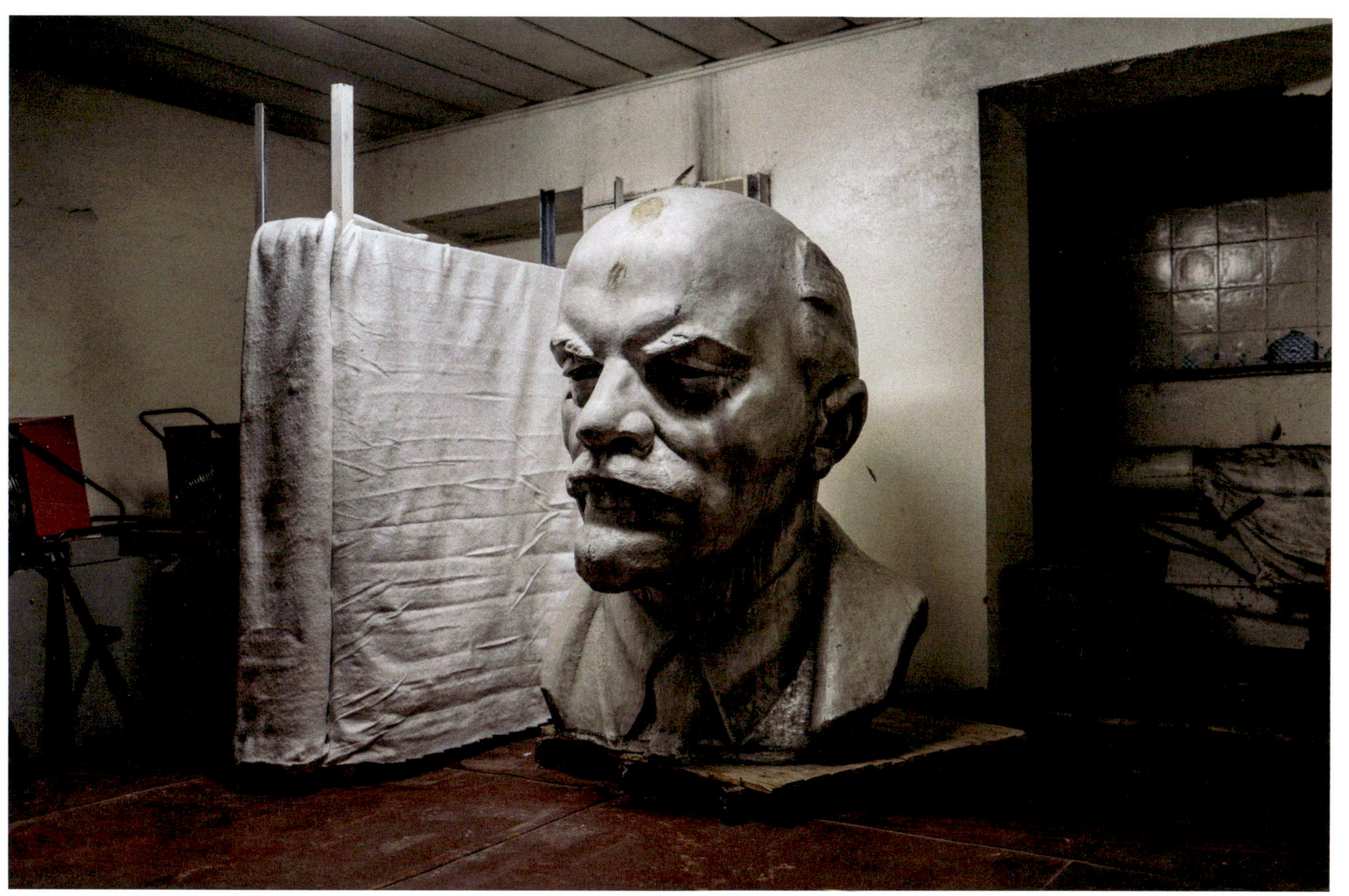

Adzhamka. 26 July 2016

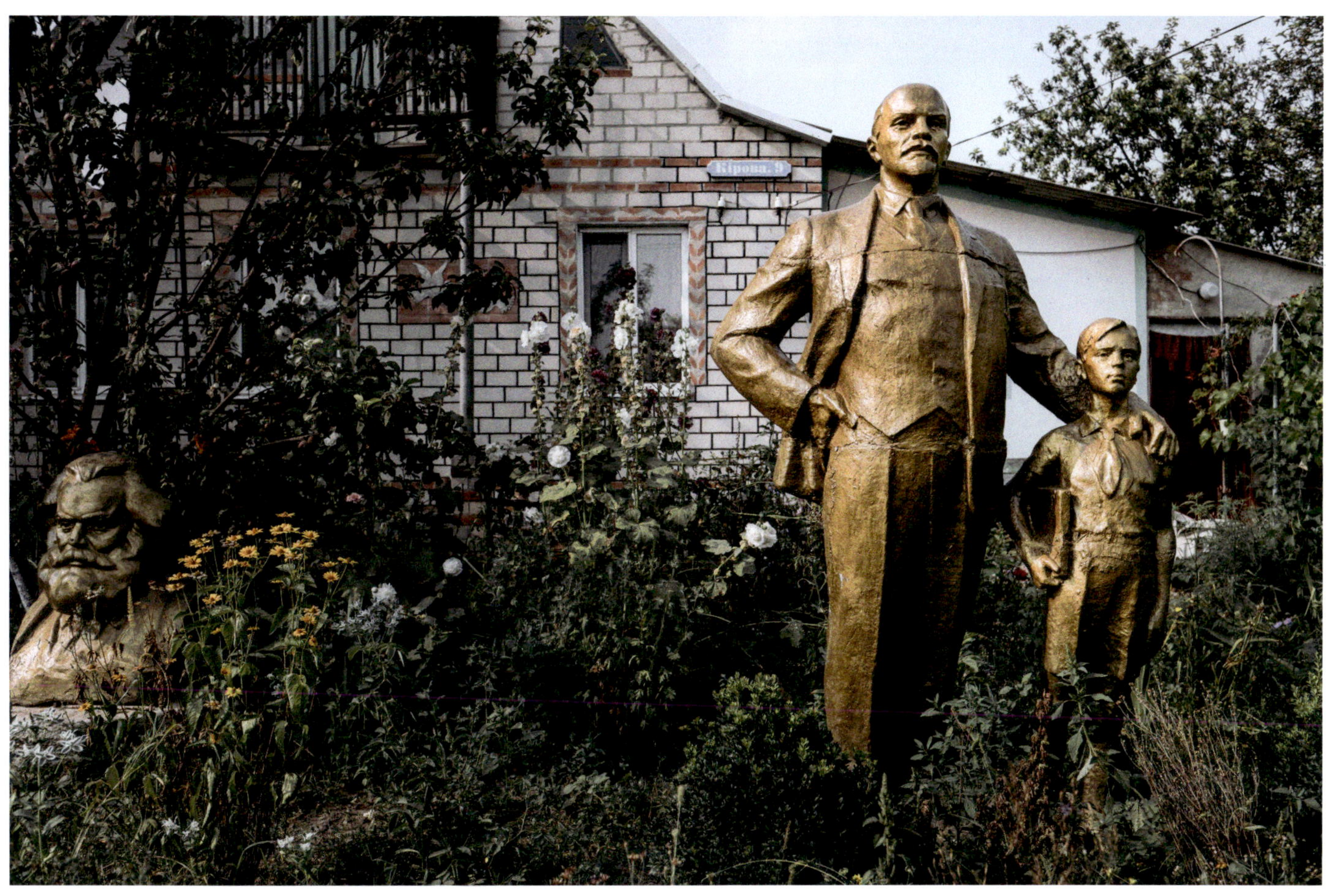
Кірова, 9

Oleksandrivka. 25 July 2016

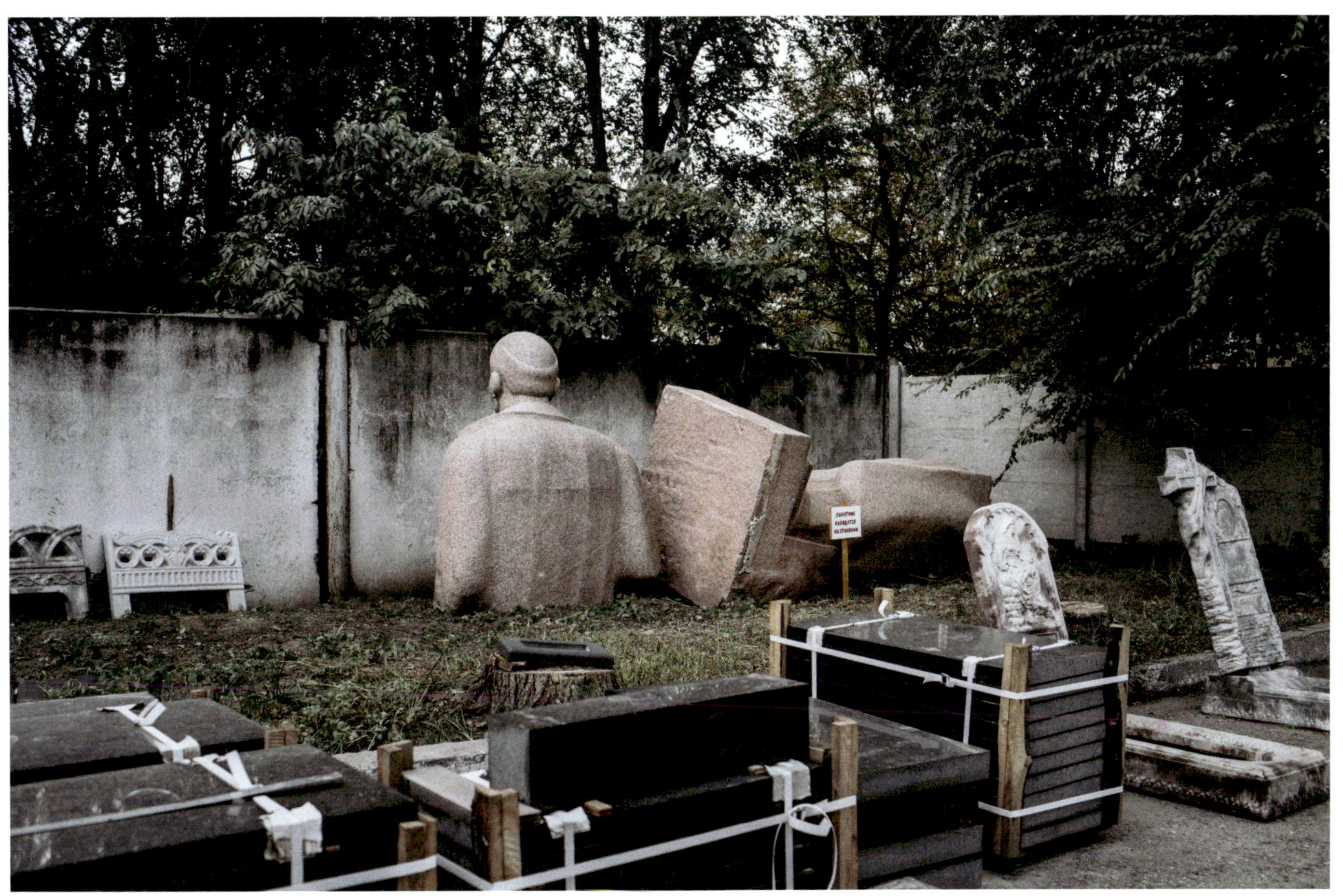

Памятник находится на хранении

Tsybuleve. 26 July 2016

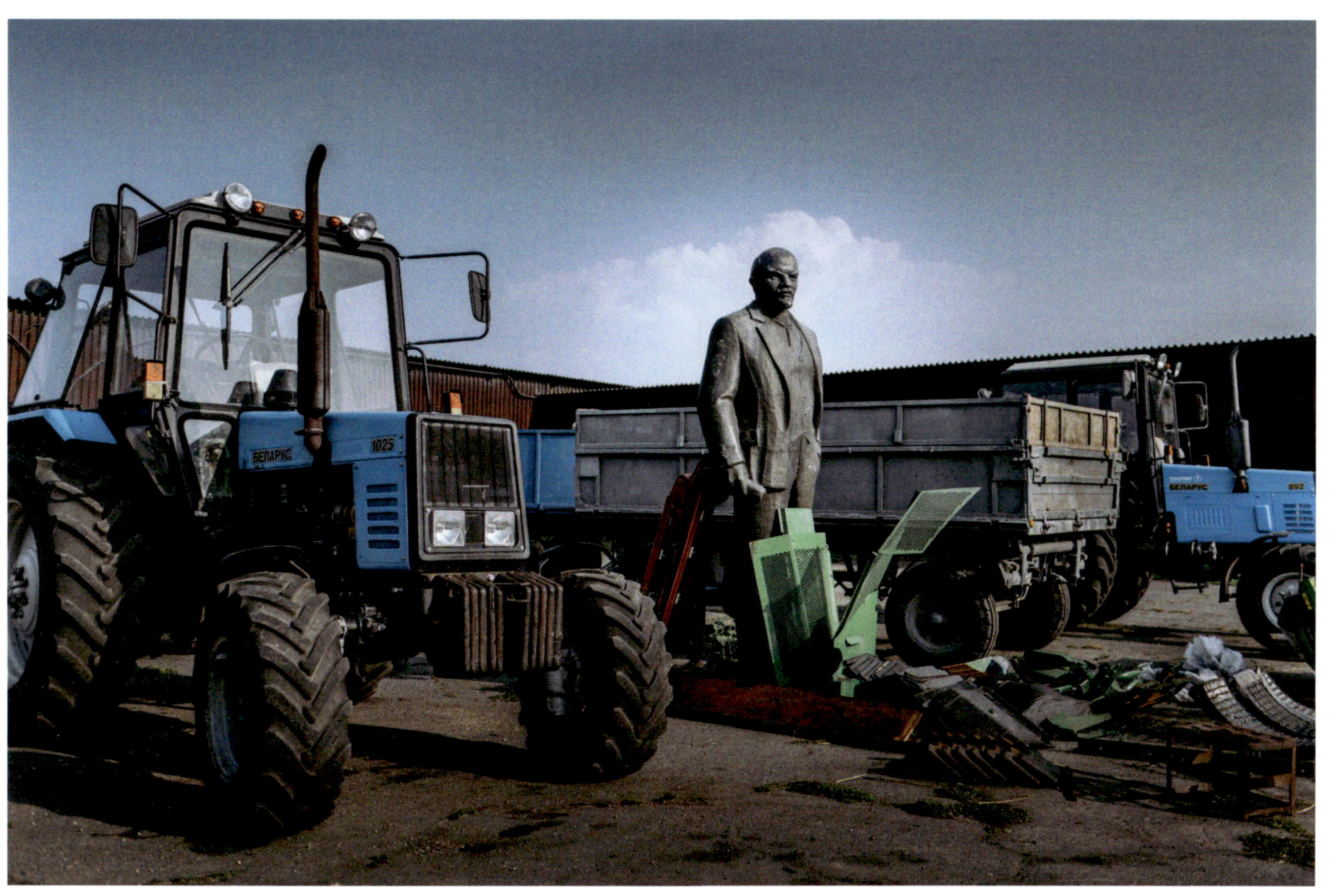
БЕЛАРУС
1025
БЕЛАРУС
892

Bar Polyana, Kyiv. 14 July 2016

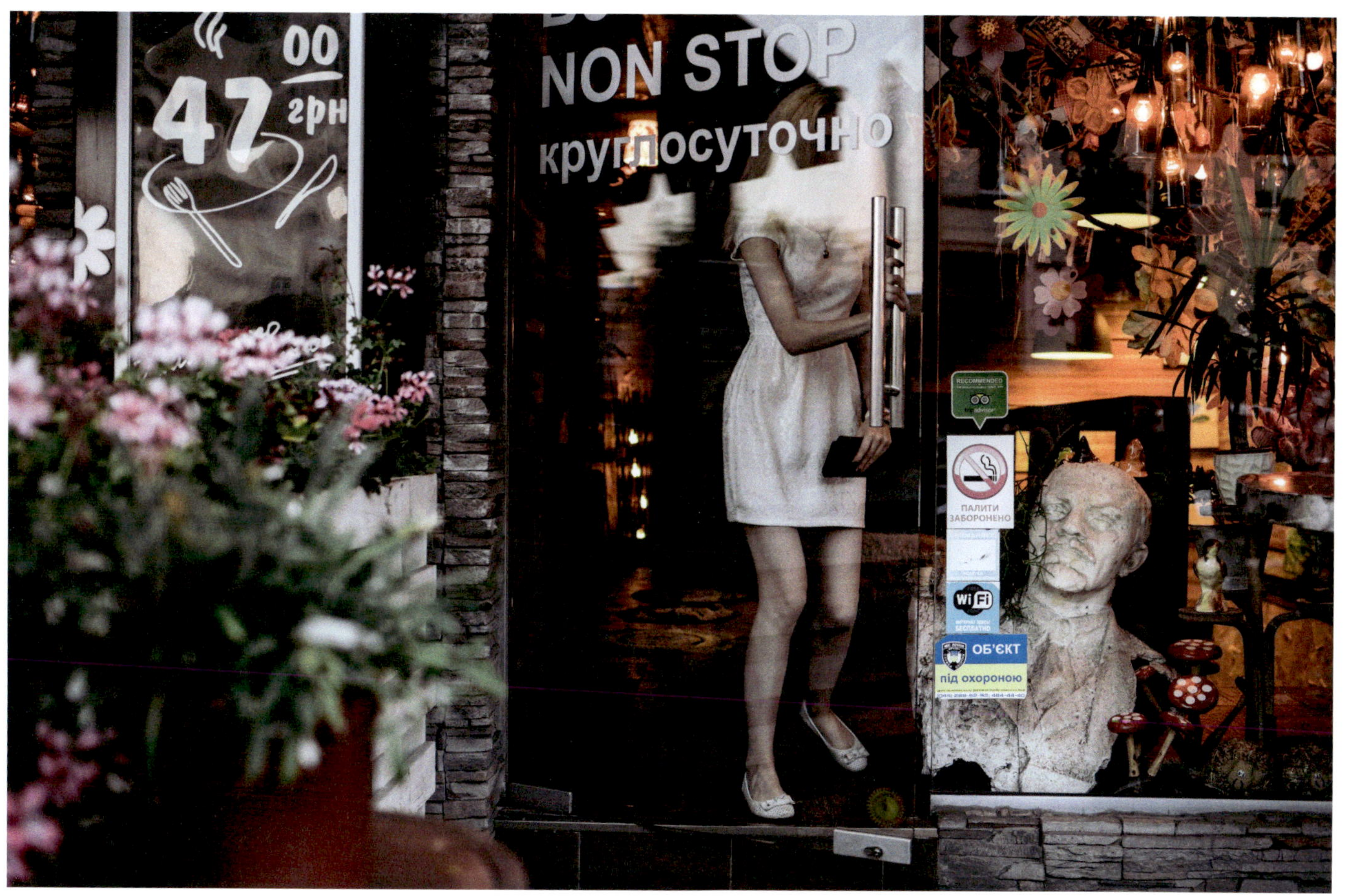
47 00 грн
NON STOP
цілодобово
ПАЛИТИ ЗАБОРОНЕНО
WiFi
ОБ'ЄКТ
під охороною
RECOMMENDED

A private collector has assembled a large number of Soviet era monuments, including dozens of Lenin statues. He stores them in his warehouse alongside materials for his glass business (also pp.130–137). Kharkiv. 2 February 2016

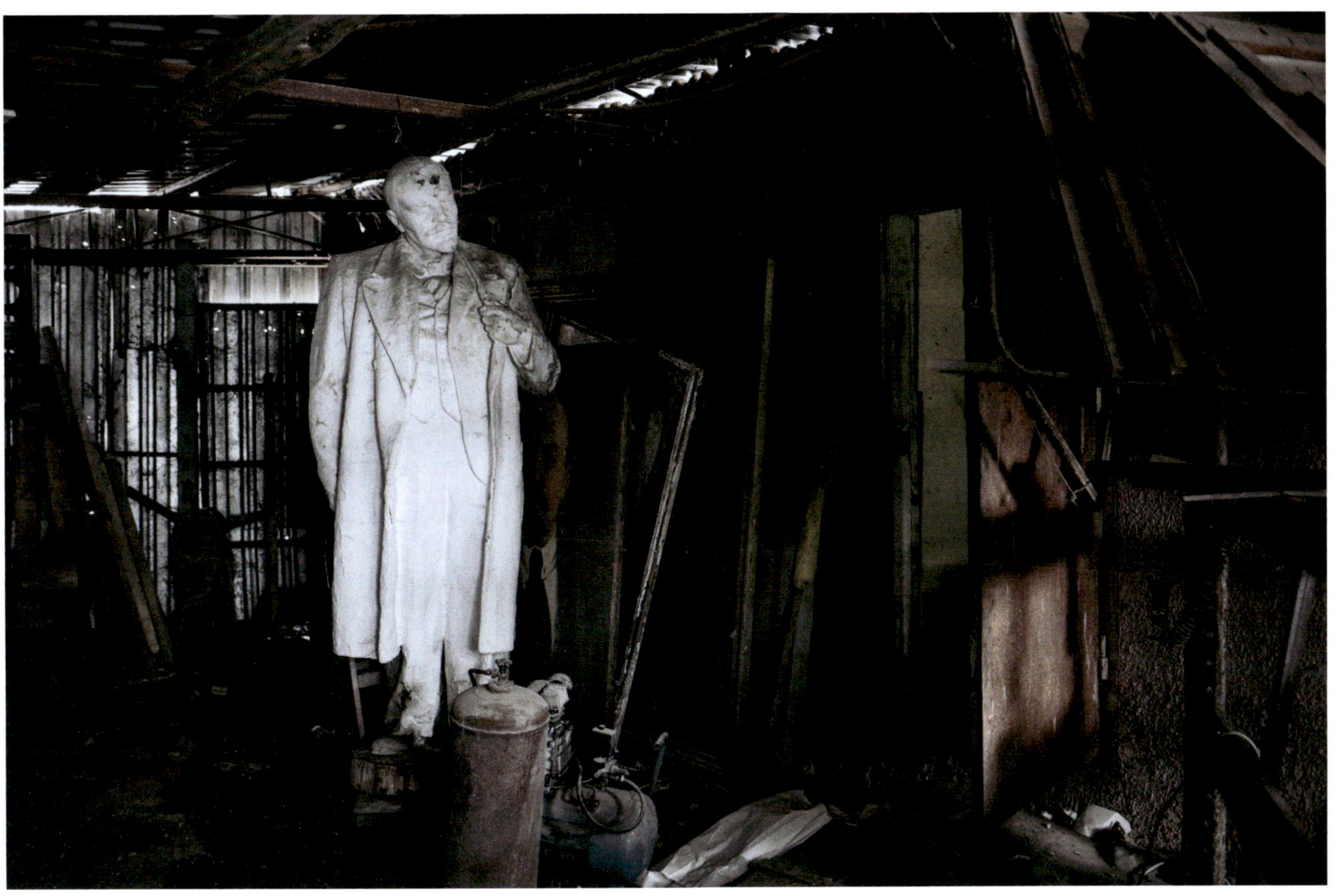

Recycled Materials Museum, Kyiv. 10 August 2016

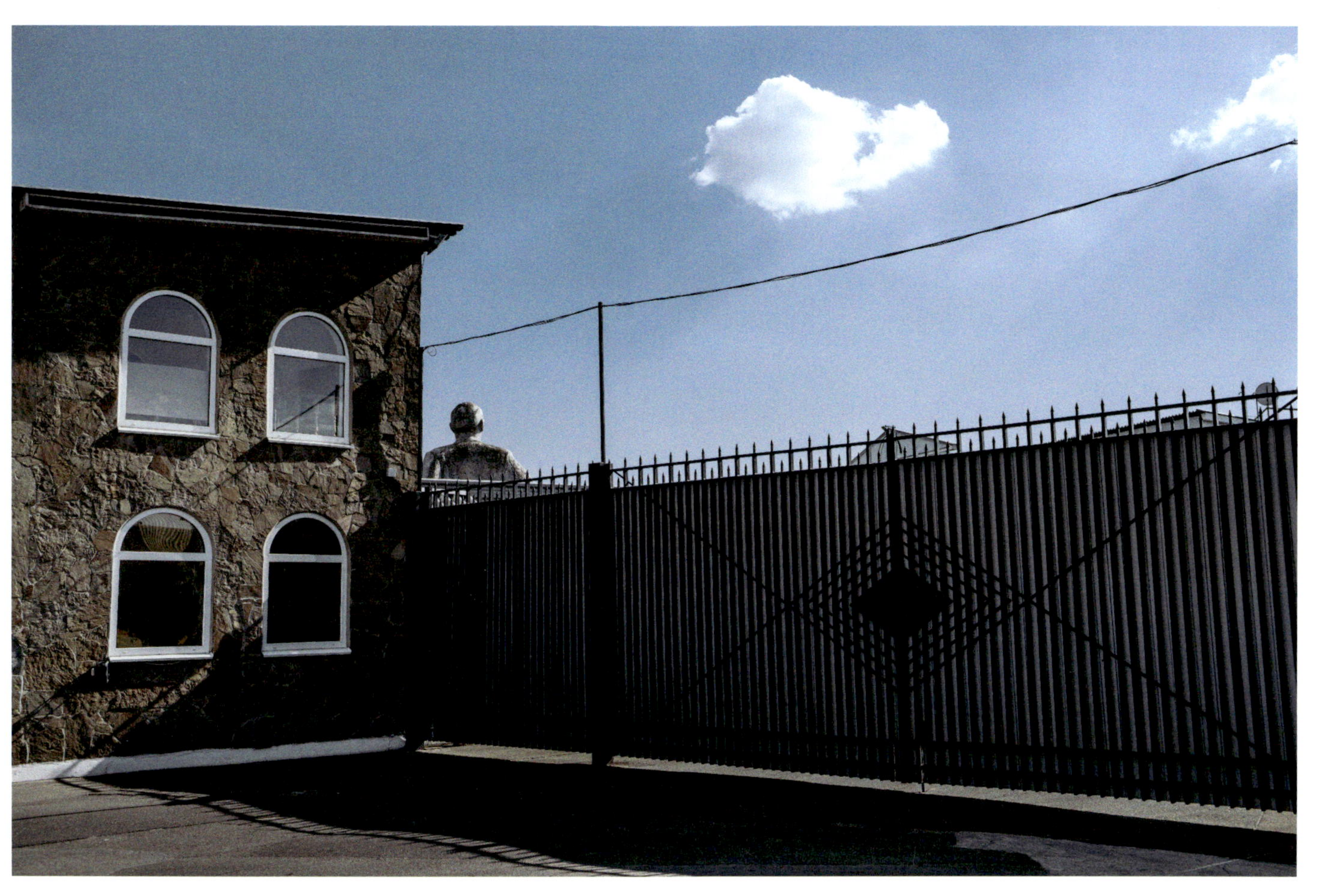

Somehow, I see him as an idealist, a guy who had these crazy ideas about the world and tried to do what he could. So much for his character. As for the monuments… Both my grandparents were Communists back in Kerch, Crimea. And every time there was a holiday or a parade, we gathered around Lenin. So for me, Lenin is associated with holidays. I never felt strongly for or against him. But it seems stupid to me to get rid of the statues for no reason. It's an important part of the past and we ought to consider that. Lenin was everywhere for so long. For many people, he has always been here. Of course, I know the history and what he did. At the same time, I don't know the history — in the sense of my family history. People don't know their own private histories, because of the totalitarian habit of keeping everything secret and making things disappear. I realise I don't know much about my grandparents and great-grandparents. Maybe they were victims of the regime, maybe not. Even now, it's hard to dig out. So… since we forgot about those things, there was no reason to love or hate Lenin. He was just here with us. The old bald guy standing on the square.

Tetyana Kozak
Journalist, Kyiv

The administration ordered us to take it down. Then we held a public consultation to find what to replace it with. People chose to have a fountain, so we have a fountain now. They use it for wedding pictures and other celebrations. Everyone calls it the 'Lenin Fountain' because it's on the exact spot where Lenin stood. So now we don't have a Lenin monument, but a Lenin fountain instead. And they call it decommunisation…

Dmytro Petrovych
Head councillor, Nova Bohdanivka

The whole debate on decommunisation is distorted. What we see now is simply a demonstration of how powerless our authorities are. Time after time, they have nothing to say, nothing to offer. They bring up issues of language, history, World War II, of who was right and who was wrong… It's obvious that this divides people – every other Ukrainian feels strongly on these issues. It's obvious that a nation won't unite under the single idea of toppling Lenin! That isn't going to assert any kind of collective political identity – Ukraine's political awareness is a well-established fact. Citizens from one end of the country to the other identify as Ukrainians in one way or another. But that doesn't matter. Ukraine has established itself as a political nation, so the issue now is to determine how and when we will define our new social contract. I believe we need to discuss the material and practical issues, in order to change people's mentalities. For the past eighty years or so, paternalism has been the normal way of life. 'Initiative is punishable' is a well-known Soviet saying, and if we want to change, then we need to change this attitude. People need to take responsibility and understand that the state should not be superior, distant and unfamiliar. It has to be understood as an extension of our collective will. Everyone has a role to play. They can topple all the Lenins they want, but only this would be real decommunisation.

Volodymyr Vorobey
Entrepreneur, Lviv

There are younger generations who don't remember anything from Communist times. They have no idea who Lenin was. It's a good thing! This criminal inheritance, this post-Soviet burden… This is not something that they have to think about. It's possible for them to build their future afresh. Older generations can't. As for the ones who miss Lenin… They gave the best years of their lives to build the USSR. They live in the past. Most of them are already pensioners, they're growing old, they'll disappear.

Ruslan Zabily
Historian and Director of the Memorial Museum Dedicated to Victims of Occupational Regimes, Lviv

Kharkiv. 2 February 2016

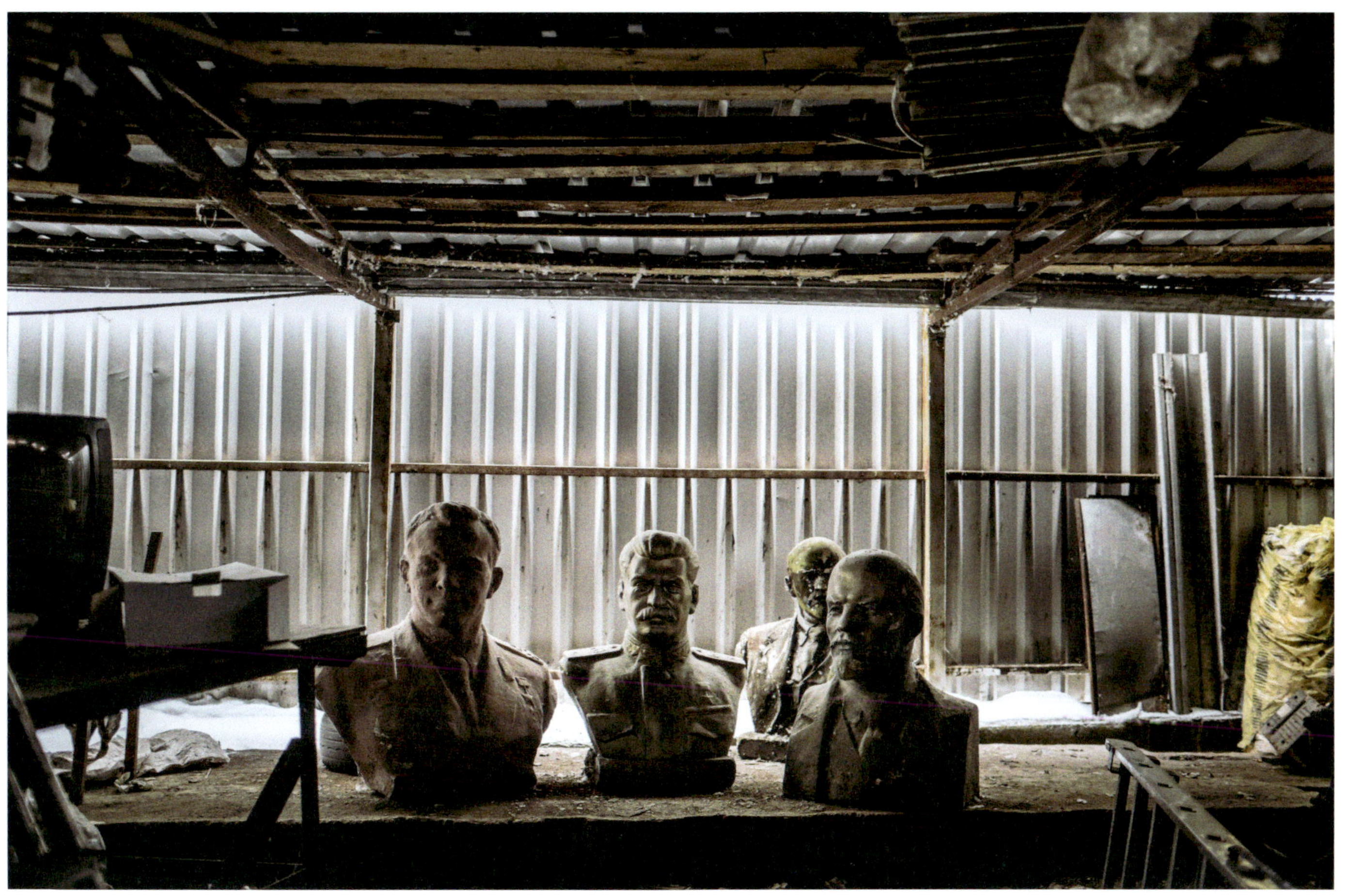

Kharkiv. 2 February 2016

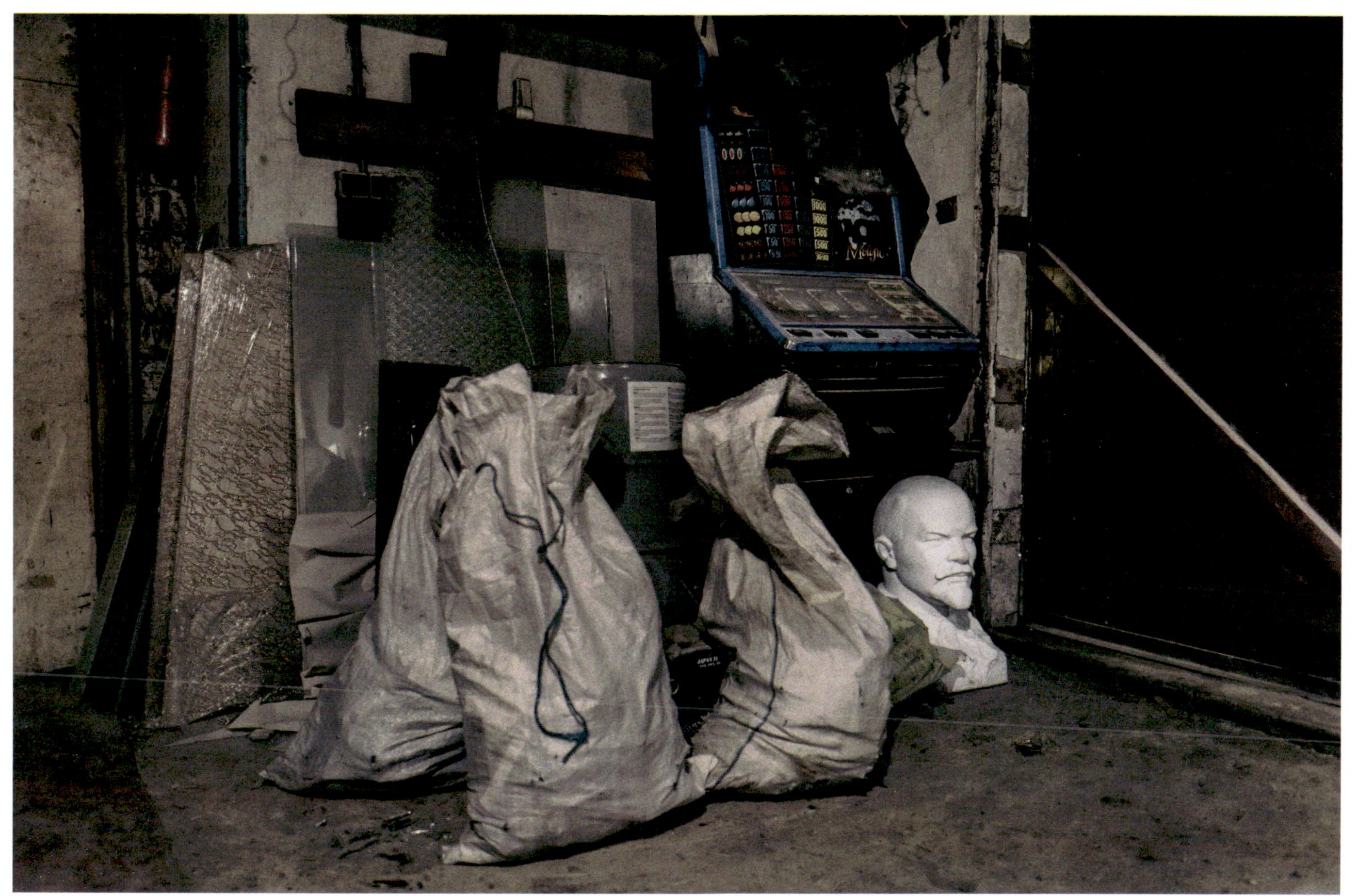

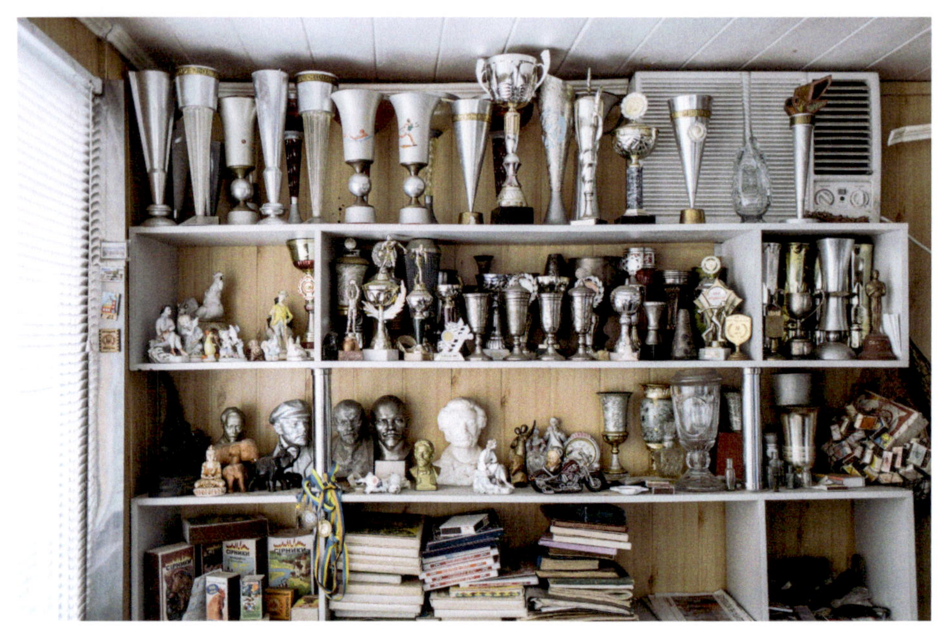

Kharkiv. 2 February 2016

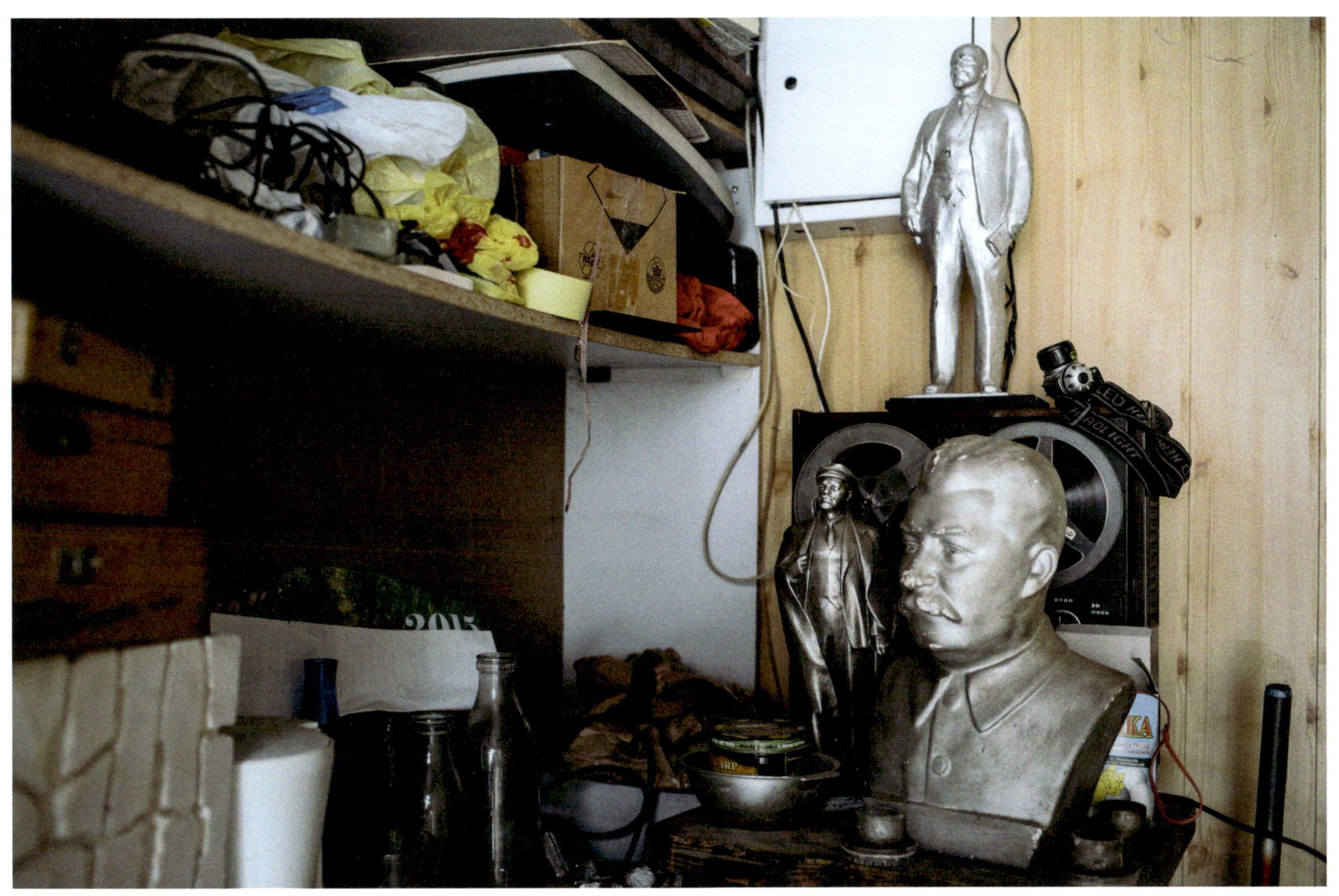

Kharkiv. 2 February 2016

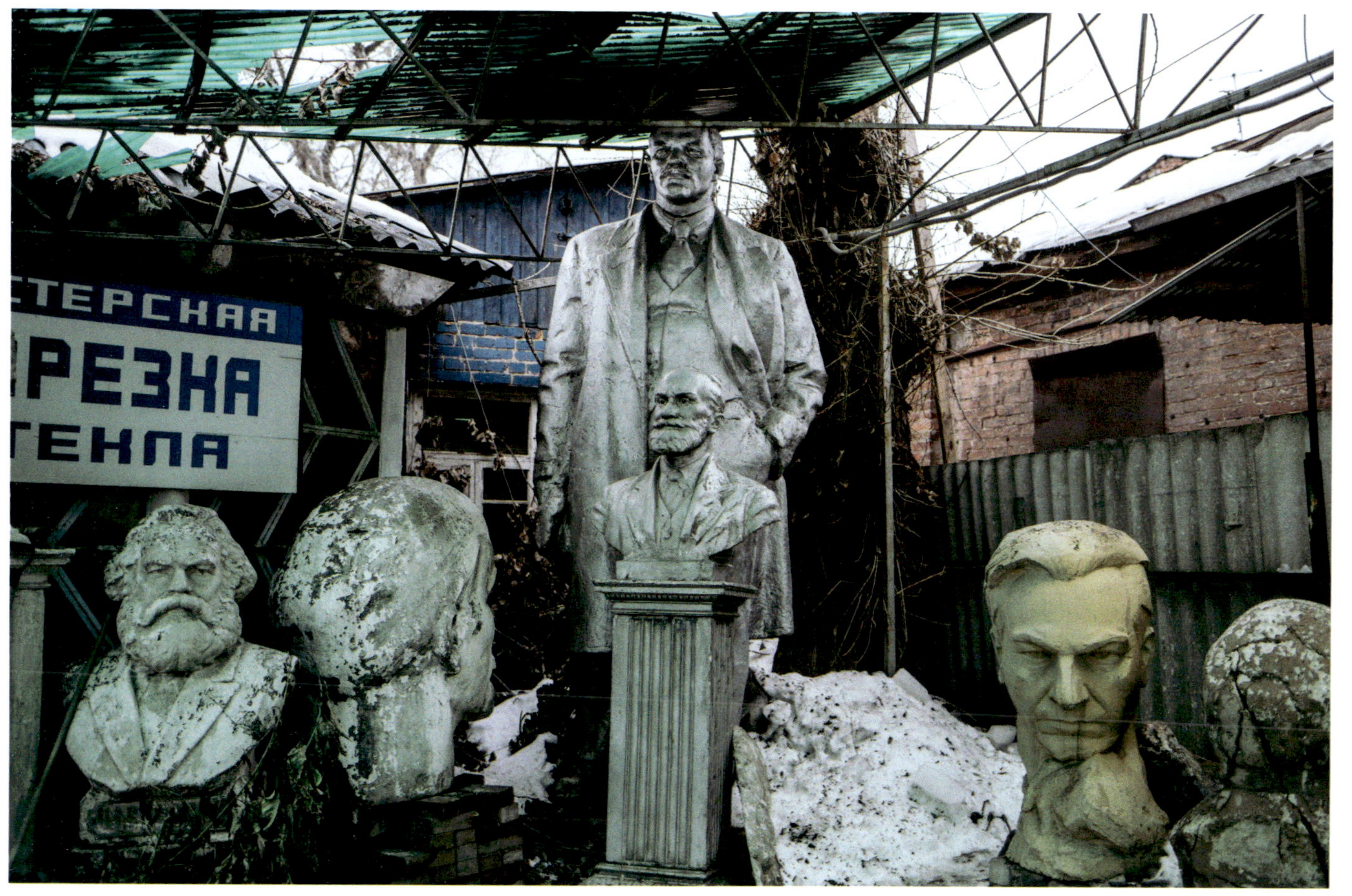
СТЕРСКАЯ
РЕЗКА
ТЕКЛА

Yosyp Bukhanchuk Fine Arts Museum, Kmytiv. 18 November 2015

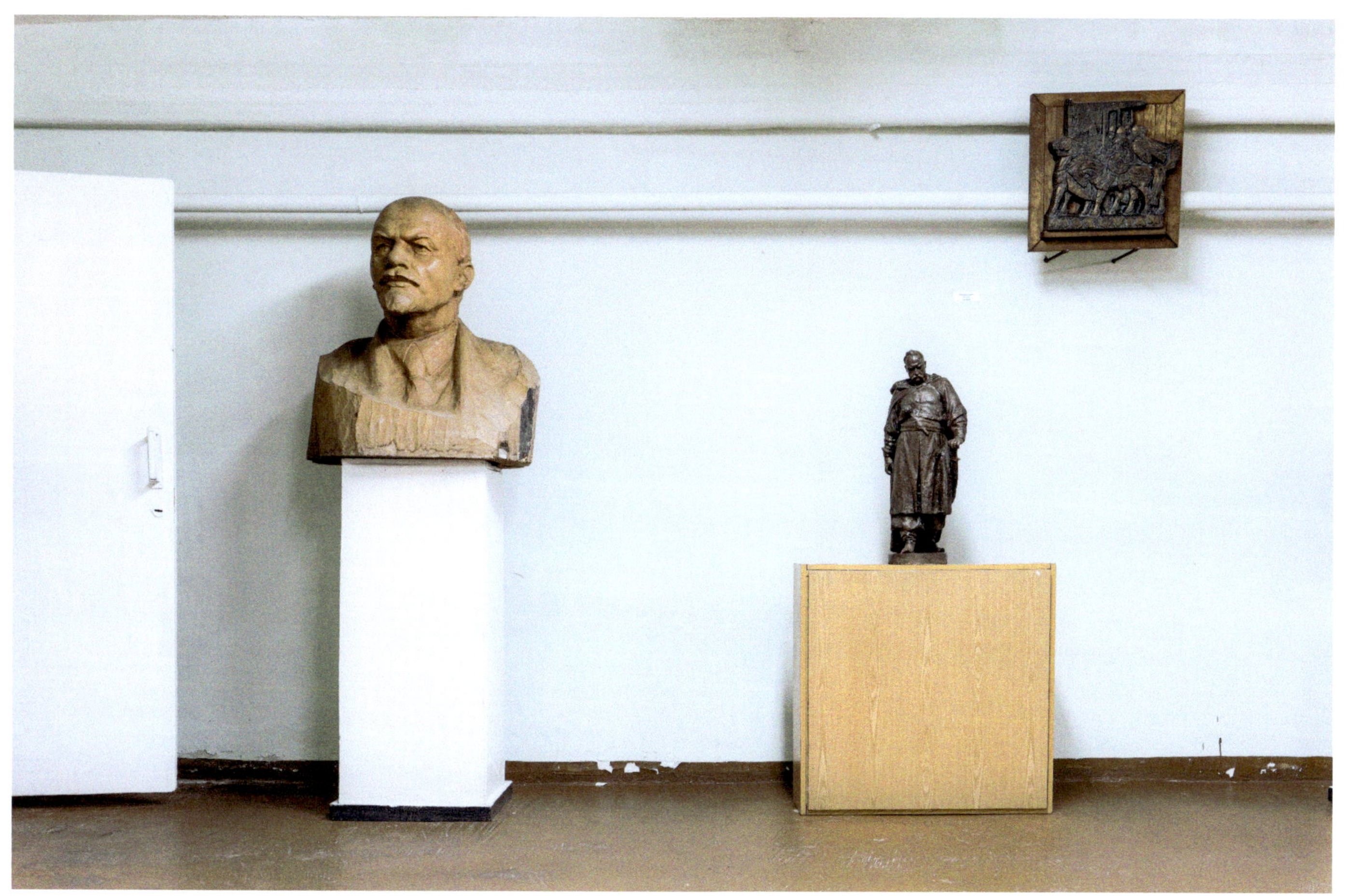

Recycled Materials Museum, Kyiv. 10 August 2016

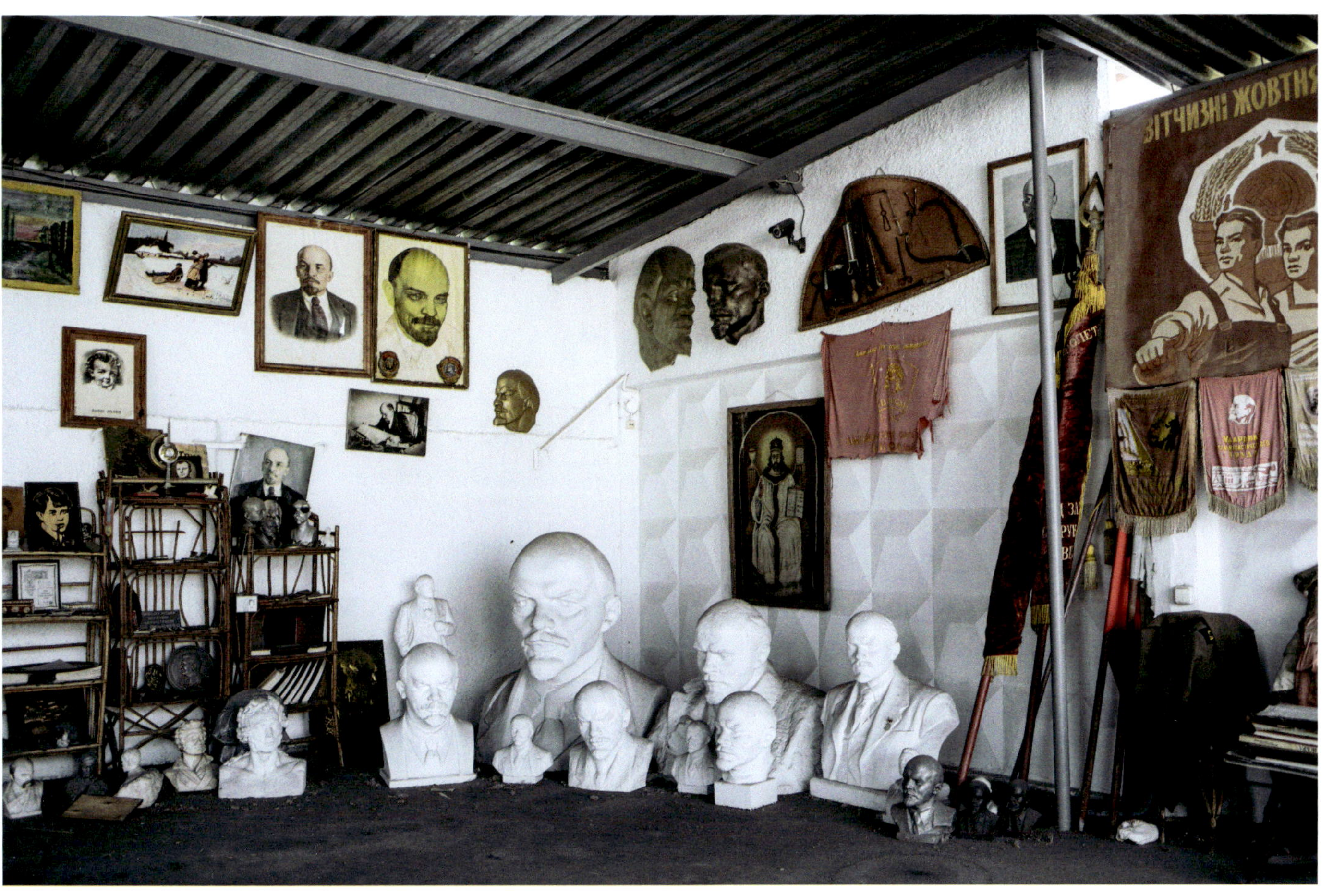

The central figure is a bust of the Soviet politician Andrey Zhdanov.
Mariupol Local History Museum, Mariupol. 1 October 2016

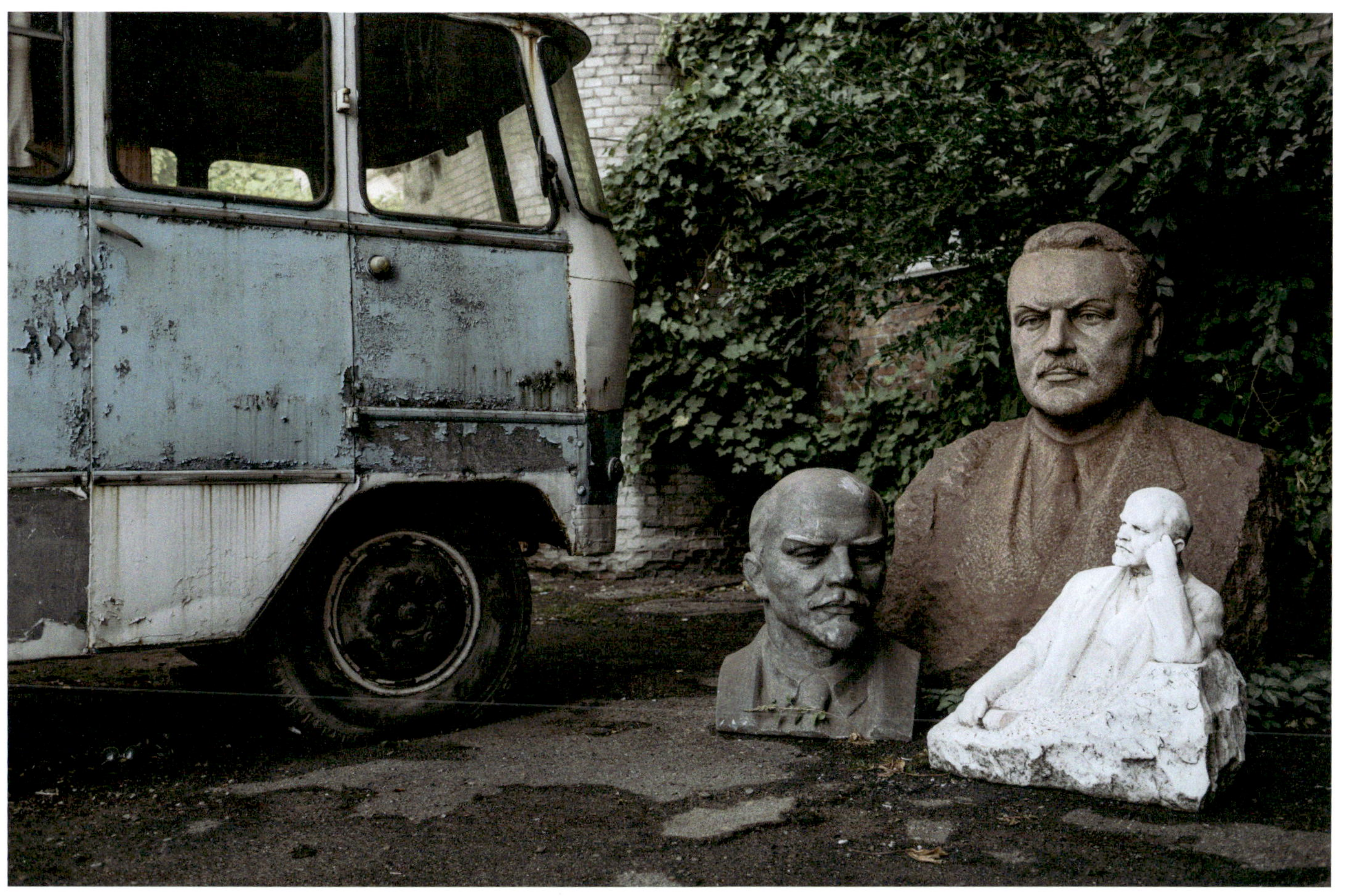

Dnipropetrovsk (now Dnipro). 24 July 2016

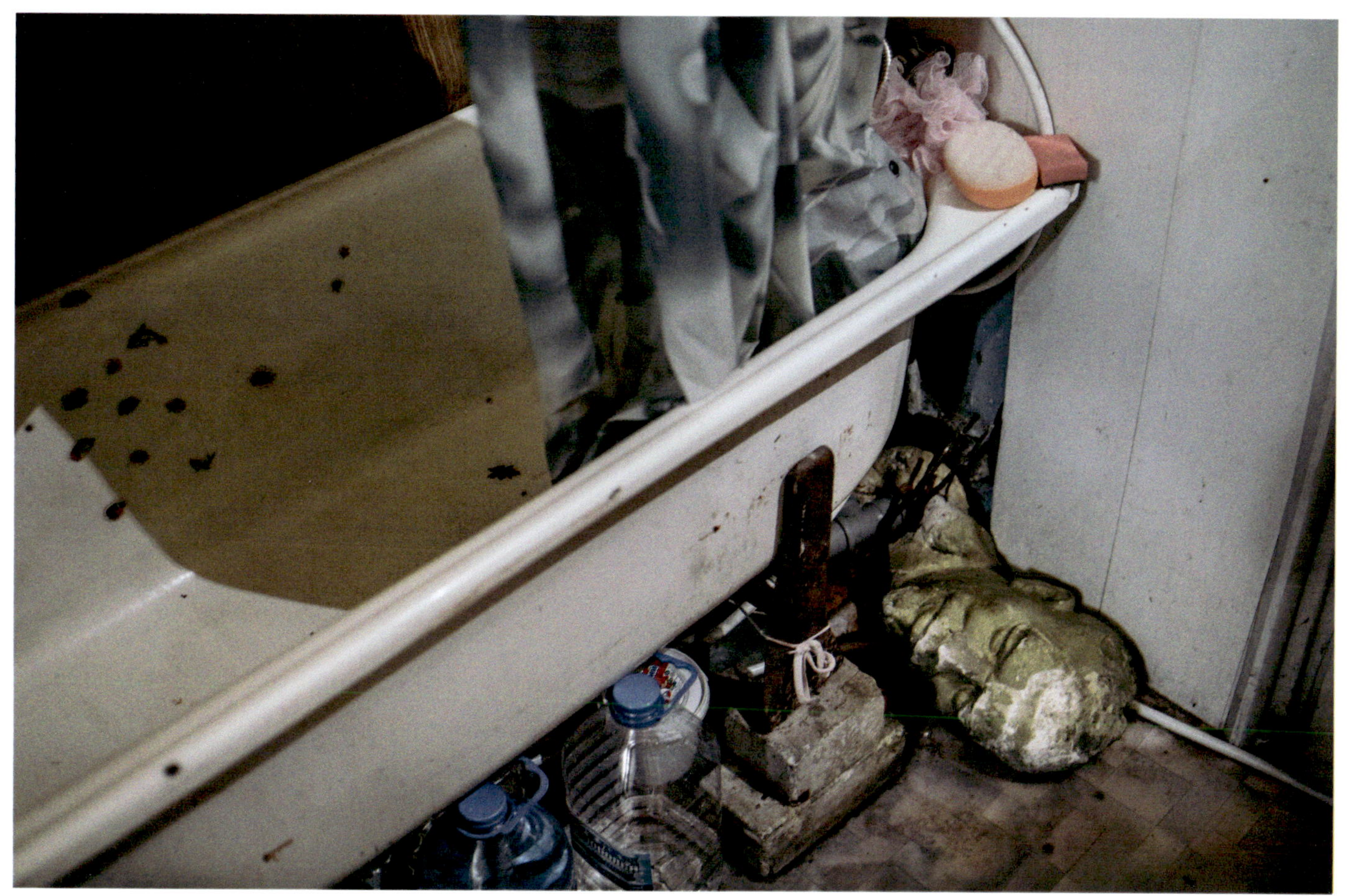

The nationalists don't like me. They ambushed me three times and tried to beat me up. They screamed that they wanted to kill me. But I'm not afraid. I served in the special forces. I went on secret operations in Mongolia, back in Soviet times. Back then, I could take on five Chinese on my own! So I'm not afraid. And I keep my Lenin in my garden. You know, I don't like the Communists, but it's a monument. Isn't it a paradox? Anyway, it's history. You want to hear another paradox? An old woman passes by from time to time, and when she sees Lenin, she crosses herself! The world is full of contradictions… Lenin is a symbol of a lost utopia. I remember that, so I understand why this is important. I tell that to these young crazy nationalists. You know what else I tell them? To go and build themselves a decent future – instead of destroying my past! Why do they care so much about Lenin that they try to tell me what to think? But they don't understand… Now they've broken it, look, the face is in pieces. I covered it with a plastic bag so they can't steal the pieces. I'll rebuild it, and display it to the neighbourhood again. And if they want to come and smash it again… I'll be waiting for them with these fists, see?

'Dyadya Kolya' (Nikolai Ivanovych)
Pensioner, Berdyansk

There are three statues of Lenin that the city administration took down. They are kept safe, but we will not show them to you – because your photography project does not depict our city or our country in a very positive light.

Tetiana
Press officer, City Administration, Melitopol

No. I can't let you see it. We had too many people coming over. And then we had scandals: the media wrote that we were asking for money just to see it. It's simply not true! We don't make money from Lenin!

Security guard
City warehouse, Mariupol

Decommunisation…? I have only one thing to say: they are waging a war against the wrong person. And we're on the frontline, so I know what I'm talking about. Now be quick, take your picture and get out of here!

Security guard
City wasteland, Volnovakha

I act as the head of this village. I took good care of our Lenin while I was ordered to do so. When the time came to take it away, I did. We always liked our statue. Lenin speaks to young pioneers – it's relaxing, harmless. But we had to take it away. Some rowdy youths had already damaged it. So a few men in the village arranged to hide it deep in the local forest. I knew about it but I wasn't involved. I tolerate it because it's like a safeguard. You know how things go in Ukraine. Over there in Kyiv, the political powers change fast. Maybe the next lot will want to put Lenin back. So we keep it. For now, everyone is OK with this little secret. They set up a table in the forest. In the evenings, they gather and drink beer by the Lenin…

Vassily Vovtchanivsky
Head of the Village Council, Horbani

We tried to take it down before, but we weren't prepared enough. We tried to approach it, but someone threw a stun grenade at us. Luckily it bounced off a bus parked nearby. Then we saw that a few thousand Berkut [a special police force known for extreme brutality under former president Viktor Yanukovych] were heading our way. So we pulled back towards Maidan. We returned on 8 December [2013]. At that time, it was unguarded because the Revolution of Dignity [also known as Euromaidan] had already gained momentum. Stanislav got up a ladder. I was holding it. He tied ropes to the head and shoulders of the statue and then a few of our guys pulled it down. It was beautiful. That was the day the revolution started. Because Lenin on Bessarabska Square wasn't just the symbol of the past, it was also a symbol of everything that was going wrong in Ukraine. So when it came down, everyone there understood it as a sign that times had changed. I keep saying that it marked the end of the 20th century in Ukraine. When it fell down, Stanislav and I took a big piece of Lenin, about 30 kilos worth. We carried it directly on to the stage at Maidan. No one there knew that Lenin had fallen. No one expected us to show up on the stage like that. It was a big shock for everyone. The whole of Maidan was so enthusiastic. This was a central act of the revolution, when people freed themselves from the past. The fights and the beginning of the war were another, a very difficult path into modernity. That's what we needed then and what we still need now: radical changes. Unfortunately, the current leadership is very soft on changes. It's even going backwards…

Eduard Leonov
Musician, Svoboda ['Freedom' Party] activist, Kyiv

The Melitopol Municipal Office is responsible for the storage of local monuments. Access to photograph them was refused despite several official letters of request, numerous phone calls and specific visits to the city administration.
Melitopol. 30 March 2016

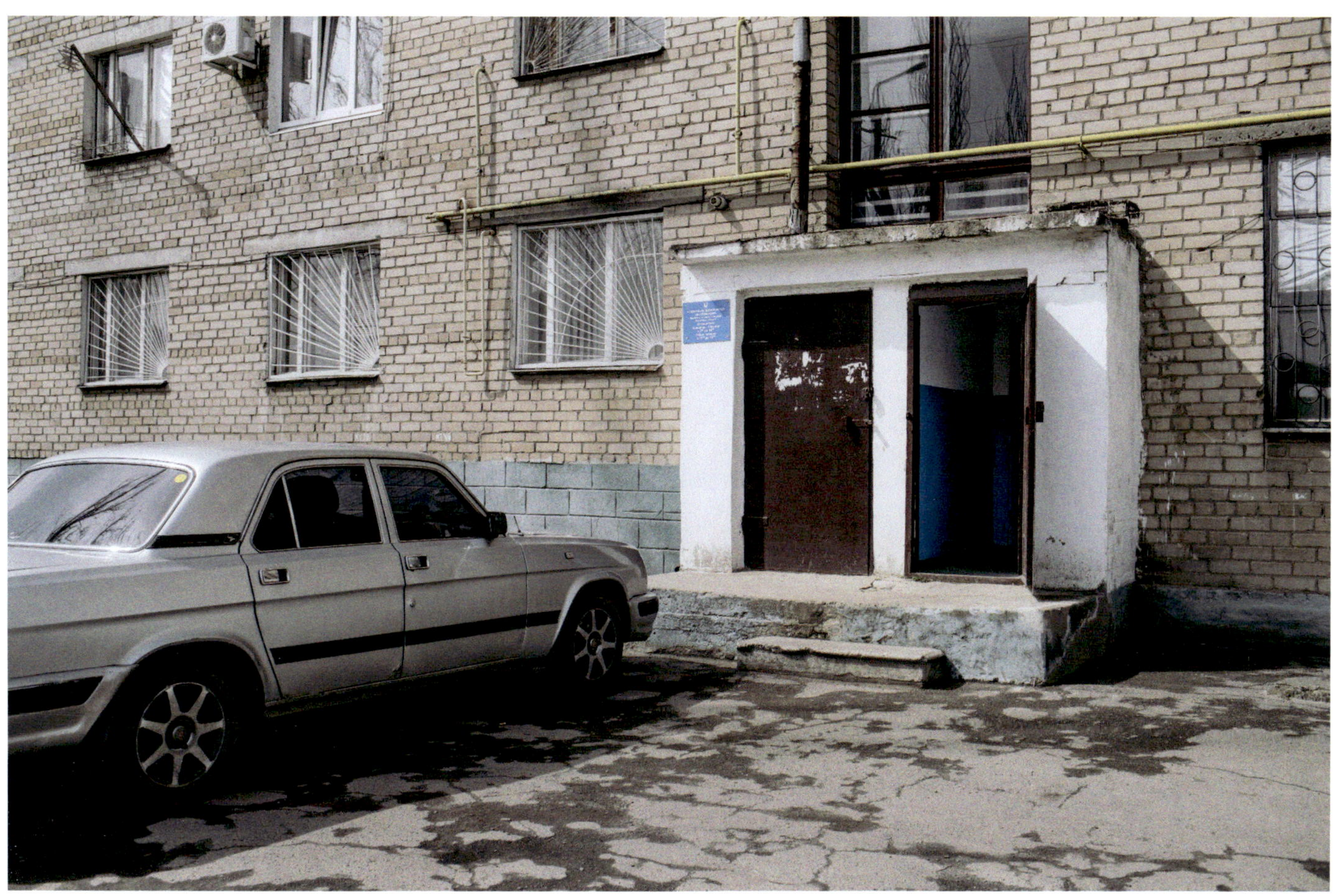

Volnovakha. 1 October 2016

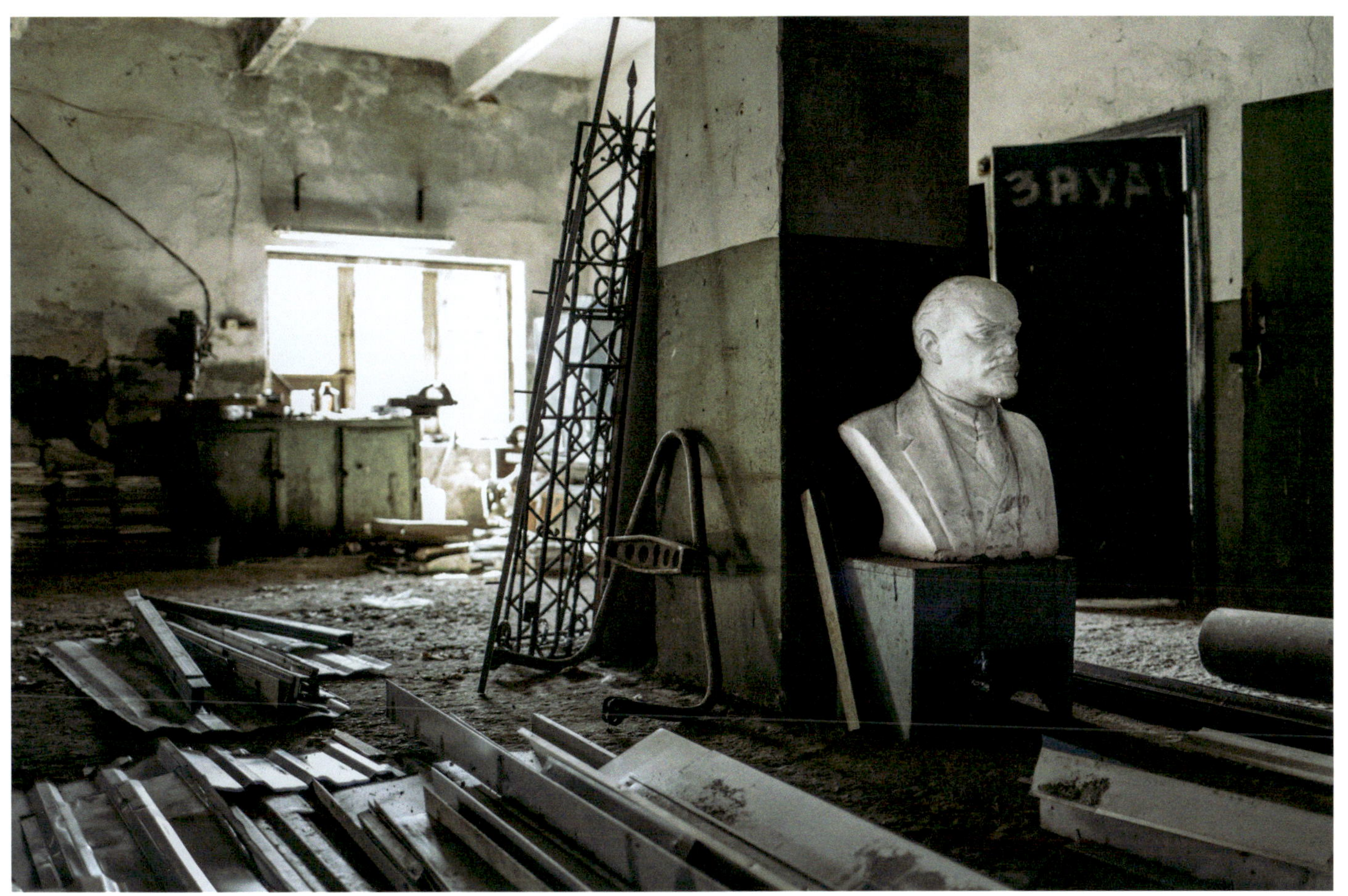

ЗАУА

Mariupol City Storage Depot, Mariupol. 1 October 2016

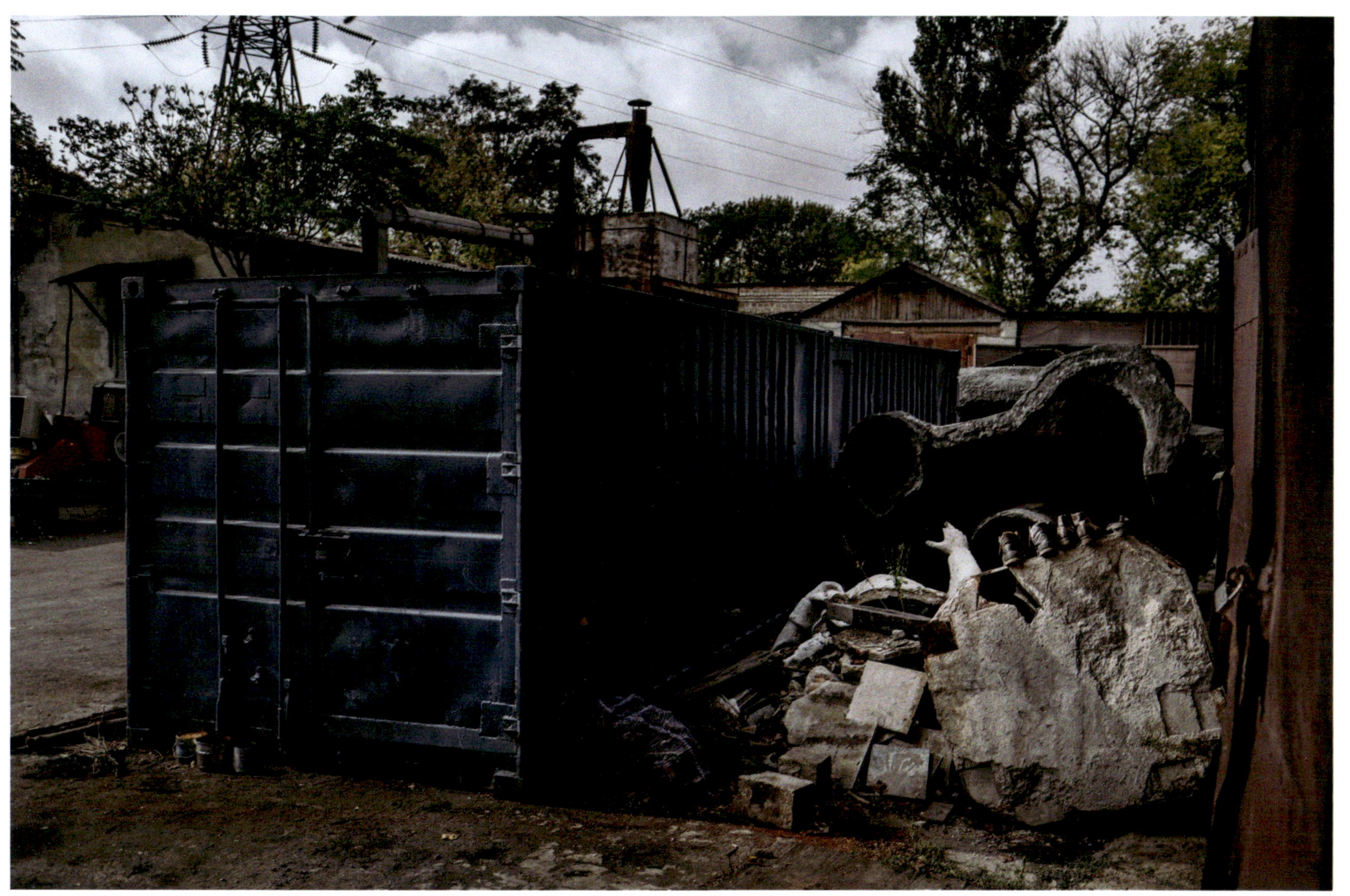

This stone Lenin bust originally belonged to a small village. It was purchased by a foreign businessman who installed it at the entrance to his residence on the outskirts of Kyiv.
Romankiv, Kyiv Region. 16 August 2016

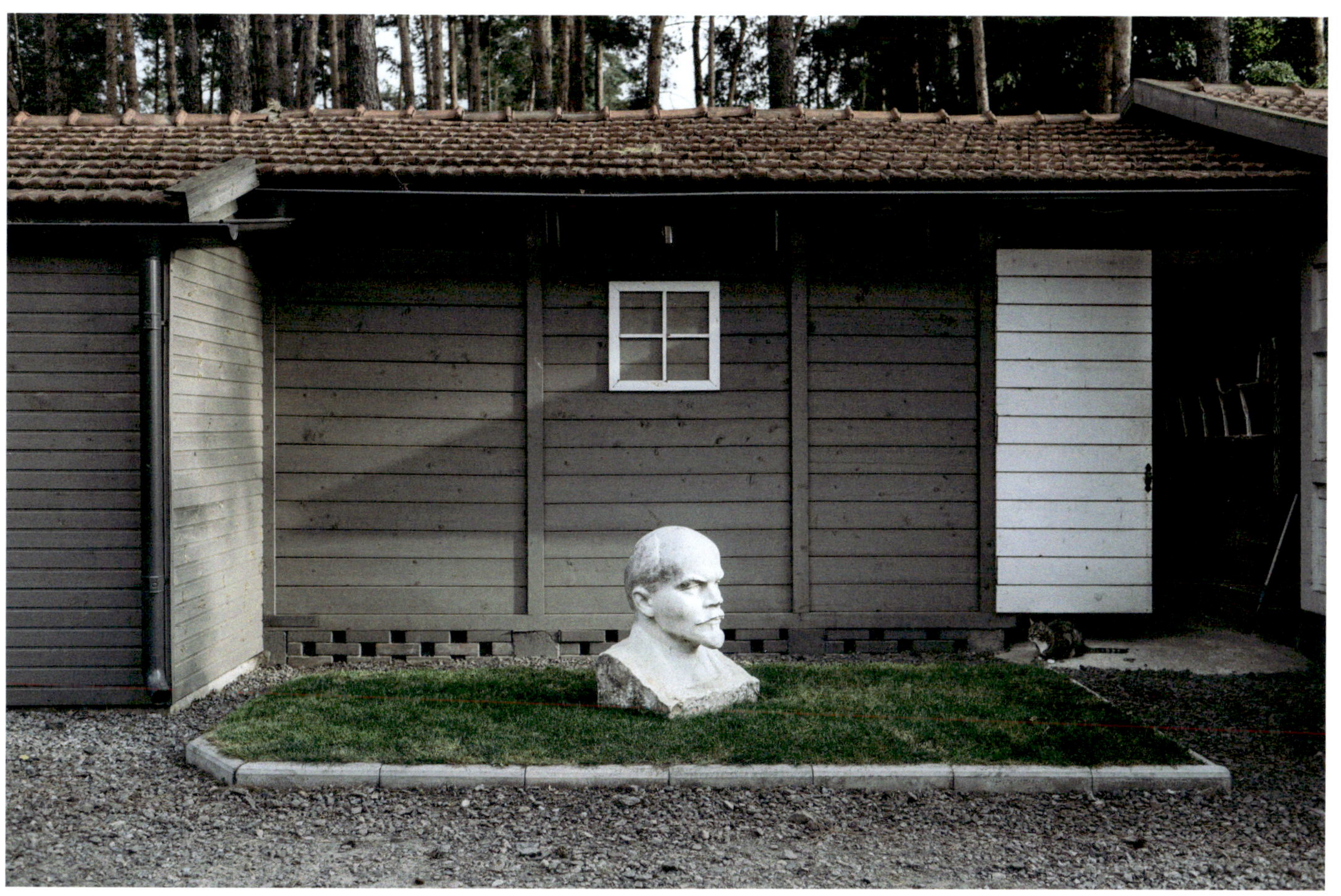

This bronze Lenin has been placed on the roof of the entrance to a building to prevent it from being
stolen and melted down for scrap.
Dniprodzerzhinsk (now Kamianske). 26 July 2016

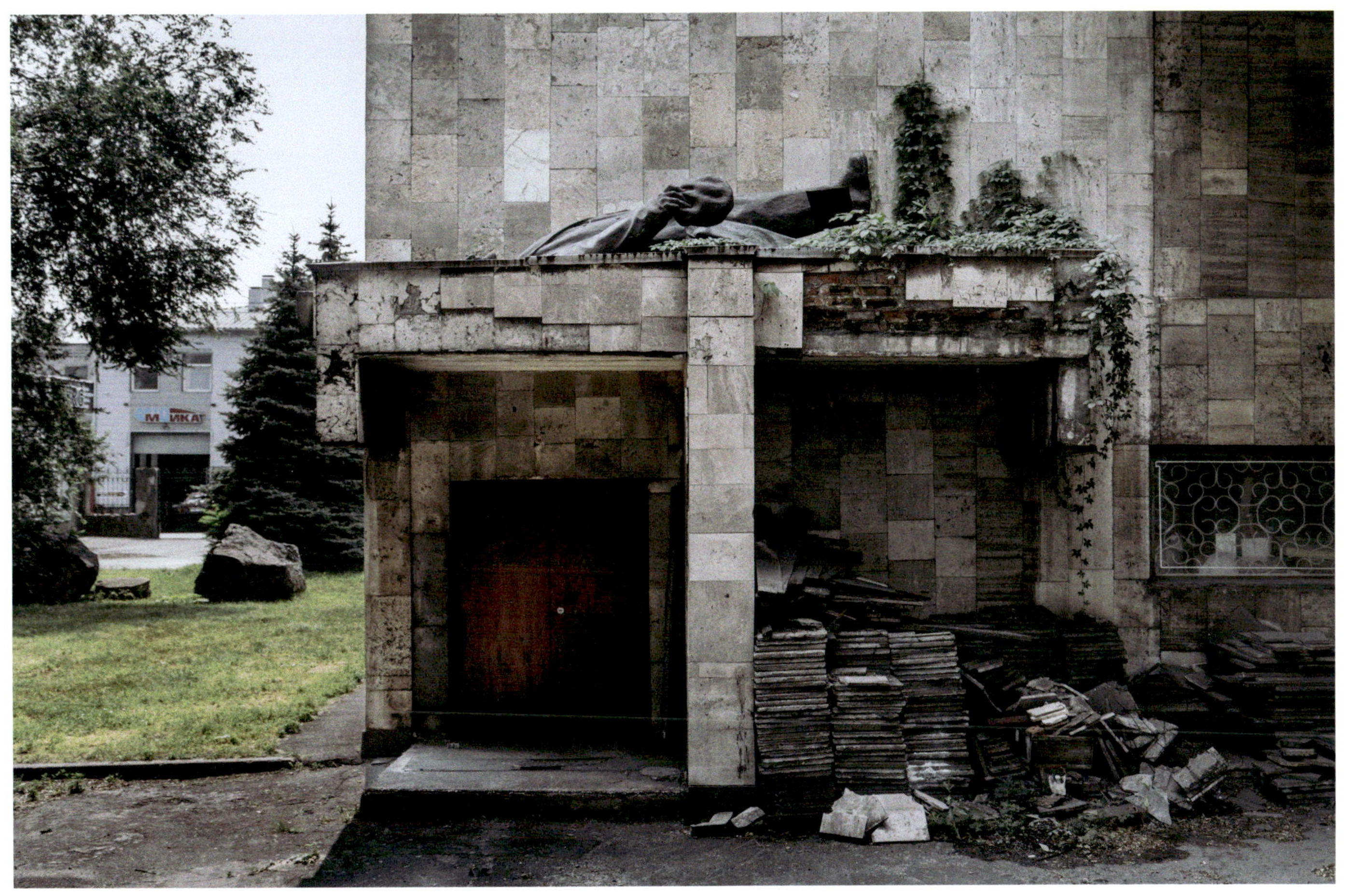

A number of the vilage residents decided to hide their Lenin monument in the forest. The mayor explained
'It's the last one in the region, and we never know what the next government will be like.' Local youths
built a table next to the statue and it became a popular place for them to gather.
Horbani, Kyiv Region. 3 July 2016

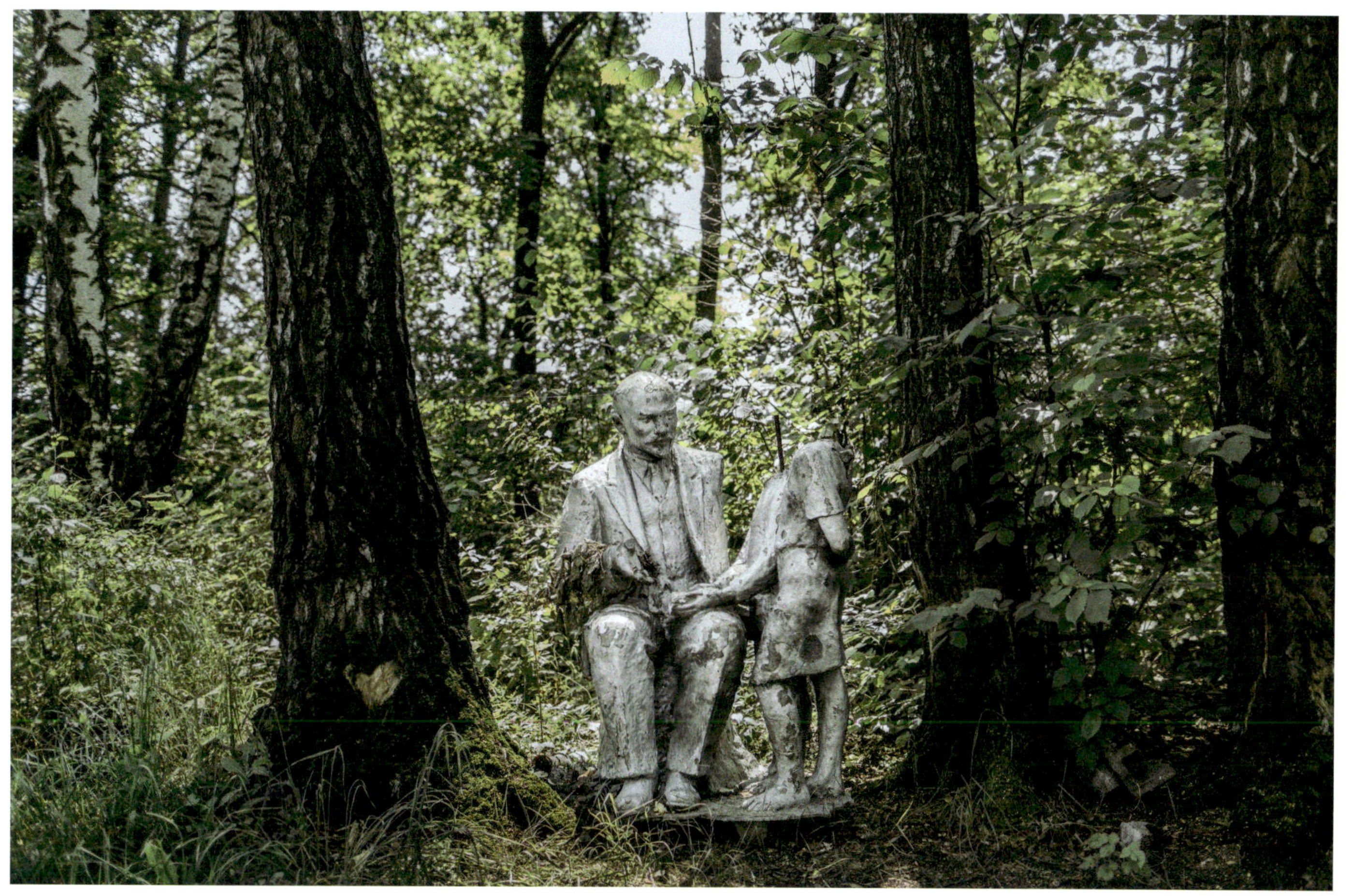

THE LENIN TRAIL

SÉBASTIEN GOBERT

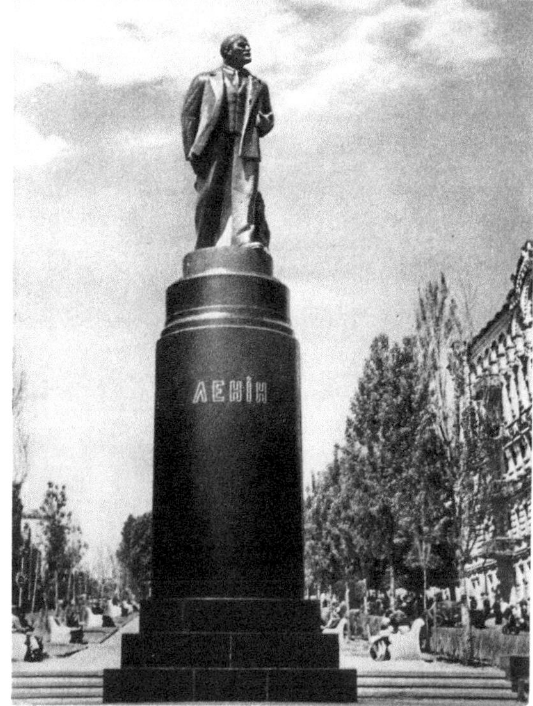

Ukrainian SSR. Kiev
Monument to V. I. Lenin
The Bessarabska Lenin statue on
Taras Shevchenko Boulevard.
Postcard, 1954

'Hey, do you know where Lenin's got to?' Niels asks, a mischievous glint in his eye.

'Which one?' Sébastien is thinking about something else. He's always distracted by something.

'The Bessarabska one, the one they demolished on 8 December.'

'I've really no idea.'

'I was thinking we could try to find it, to see what they did with it? They were so aggressive during the Euromaidan protests… I wonder what it looks like now? I'd like to photograph it. The two of us could go looking for it together. What do you think?'

Sébastien looked up. He saw the glint. 'That's a great idea! Yeah, why not?'

That's how it all started. The Lenin hunt. Two friends chatting in a bar. Two Westerners fascinated by Ukraine, but tired of covering the endless string of events that had rocked the country since November 2013. The Lenin hunt seemed like a playful way to break the daily grind of war reporting while doing something interesting at the same time. After all, this was the Bessarabska Lenin we were talking about!

THE FALL IS EVERYTHING

On 8 December 2013 the Euromaidan unrest was particularly violent. It was impossible to determine who was winning the confrontation between the demonstrators and President Viktor Yanukovych's authoritarian regime. That is until a handful of protestors, most of them linked with the nationalist Svoboda ('Freedom') Party, invaded Bessarabska Square and pulled down the Lenin statue, attacking it with hammers.

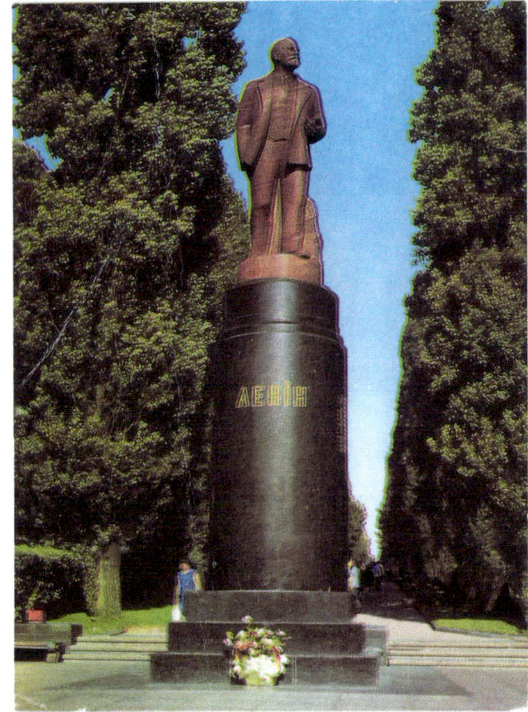

Aeroflot Soviet Airlines
By Aeroflot to Kiev!
Kiev. Monument to V. I. Lenin.
Postcard, 1976

Niels was eating pizza in Kyiv at the time. When he saw the events unfolding on a nearby television screen, he was reminded of the fall of the Berlin Wall. He rushed directly to the scene. Sébastien was on a beach in Barcelona when he received a text message with the news. He'd hoped to spend a few days in the sun after several demanding weeks in Ukraine, but the next day he was on a plane back to Kyiv. For years, the regime had protected this Lenin, body and soul. If it had fallen, it meant that Yanukovych was much weaker than anyone had imagined. Lenin wasn't important in himself but, with his fall, something had changed. So, pizza or beach, everything had to be dropped.

Months later – after regime change, the annexation of Crimea, division in Donbass, a Boeing downed, millions of lives shattered and countless certainties buried – the fall of Lenin remained just as important. The fall of the Lenins, in fact. The 'Leninopad', as it was officially termed, had swept away dozens of monuments all over the country, in a chaotic effort to break with the past and, accordingly, with Russia. The so-called decommunisation laws of May 2015 had tried to provide a framework for the movement. But rather than offering answers, they raised only questions. What was decommunisation? Why? What comes next? Where had all the Lenin statues seized from public spaces actually ended up? What do Ukrainians want to do with these vestiges of the past? What do they want to do with their past as a whole? And the Bessarabska Lenin, which had aroused such passions, where was that?

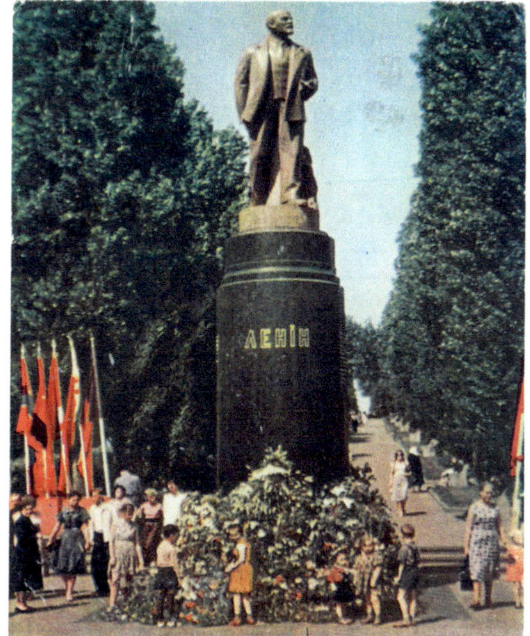

Kiev Today. Monument to V. I. Lenin.
Postcard, 1962

FIRST LEADS

'A Svoboda activist has got Lenin's hand,' a friend tells us. Ah! This is a start. Of course, it would nice to find the body too. With a big block of red quartzite like that, there has to be something left. But it's OK, we'll start with the hand. Eduard Leonov is the activist's name: a singer, a former member of parliament, a patriot with a Cossack haircut. Nice portrait. But he's not answering his phone, despite our repeated calls. We try his assistant. 'Mr Leonov is in prison for two months.' Ah. 'Try Lviv, in Western Ukraine. The hand might be there.' Lviv, with its cobbled streets, its Austro-Hungarian façades and its elegant cafés: a good opportunity for a relaxing weekend, as well as to meet with a local Svoboda activist. 'The hand is not here, who told you that?' Ah, well. False lead.

In that case, we may as well go straight to the source. The statue is municipal property and so Kyiv town hall must have some idea of its whereabouts. An obvious thought. But after checking with Mayor Vitali Klitschko's team, it appears it's not so clear-cut. We even get the impression we are bothering them when we ask what has happened to this communal possession… Let's try another direct source.

Volodymyr Viatrovych, director of the Institute of National Remembrance, is the pope of decommunisation. He may have an idea. We set out to meet him one chilly autumn evening. 'No, I haven't a clue. But I can try to find out.' From his sofa, Viatrovych picks up the phone and calls a contact, an old historian friend. Who gives him the number of an artist in a village not far from Kyiv.

163

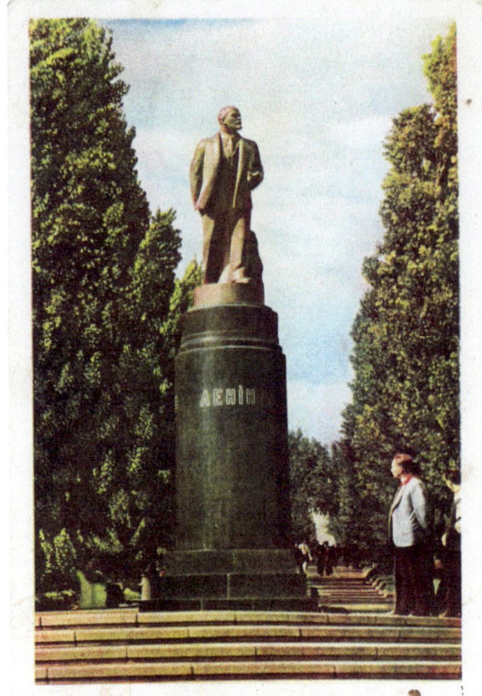

U.S.S.R. Kiev, capital of the Ukrainian Republic. Monument to Lenin.
Postcard, 1973

'Right, it's all sorted. Take his details and go and see him whenever you want. Any other questions?' Viatrovych leaves quickly. A man in a hurry, like any other historian who is very much concerned with the present. His office in Kyiv was once the headquarters of the Cheka, the bloody secret police of the early Soviet years; it is from here that he is boldly leading the country's decommunisation campaign. So, a man in a hurry, but efficient with it. Looks like we've got what we want.

'The Lenin is in the garden next door. But I forbid you to go there, or to talk to the owner. Don't mention my name either — I'm his tenant and he might throw me out if he finds I've been talking to you. He's very cautious.' The edginess of the artist in this country village sets us thinking. Why such wariness about protecting Lenin? The statue has fallen — why does the collector need to keep it secret? Unless he's not supposed to have it? Yes, that must be the answer. It is municipal property, after all. And, as a private collector, he can't show it in public. So we have to be very careful about how we contact him. This Lenin hunt is much more intriguing than we expected. By that point, we had found and photographed many Lenins, but the mystery surrounding this one confirms its value, and the importance of our investigation.

On the day of our appointment, it is not the collector who greets us. Vyacheslav is his assistant, a big, moustachioed man with piercing eyes. After the obligatory tour of hordes of uniforms and paintings dating back to the 16th century, we start talking about

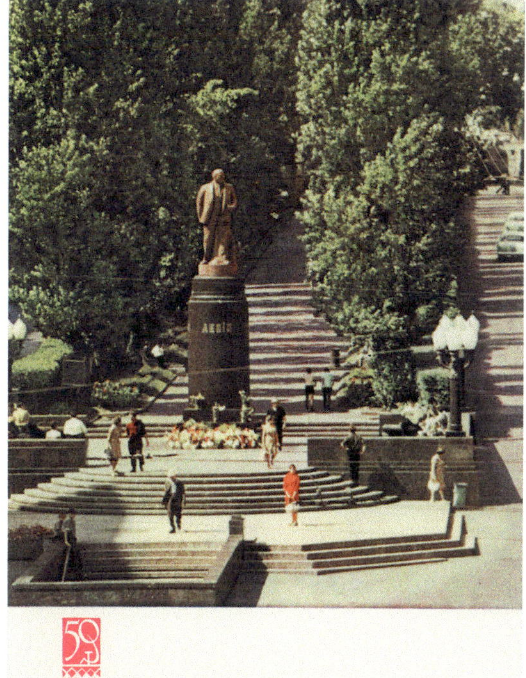

Kiev, the capital of the Ukrainian SSR
Monument to V. I. Lenin.
Sculptor S. Merkurov.
Postcard, 1967

the manipulation of history, from the Cossacks to decommunisation. It's a very general conversation, but it leads Vyacheslav to deliver the magic words: 'We know where Lenin is.' He invites us to see it, to photograph it. And since we are going to be meeting again, could we buy a book published in France and have it delivered to him? That would be much appreciated. Just as we are getting ready to leave, the chief collector turns up at the office. Another man in a hurry. The kind who doesn't look you in the eye when he shakes your hand. But never mind. Things seem to have gone smoothly. Our search is reaching its conclusion.

LESSONS FROM DECOMMUNISATION

By early 2016, our project was well under way. We had decided to go beyond our initial curiosity and to extend our Lenin search. According to the statistics, in 1991 there were more than 5000 statues of Lenin in the Soviet Socialist Republic of Ukraine. Given the size of the territory, that represented the highest density of Lenins in the entire Soviet Union. So there was lots to be done. Over several trips we had discovered statues in a variety of situations and positions, each illustrating, in its own way, a facet of the continuing decommunisation. We had met scores of people who wanted to discuss the subject. The name 'Lenin' loosened tongues: for, against, indifferent, nostalgic, vindictive – everyone had an opinion about Dyadya Vova (Uncle Vlad). Everyone had their own experience of the fall, and their own understanding of decommunisation. Ultimately, the process became illegible.

On the 1 May holiday! [International Worker's Day, a public holiday in the former Soviet Union]
Postcard, 1974

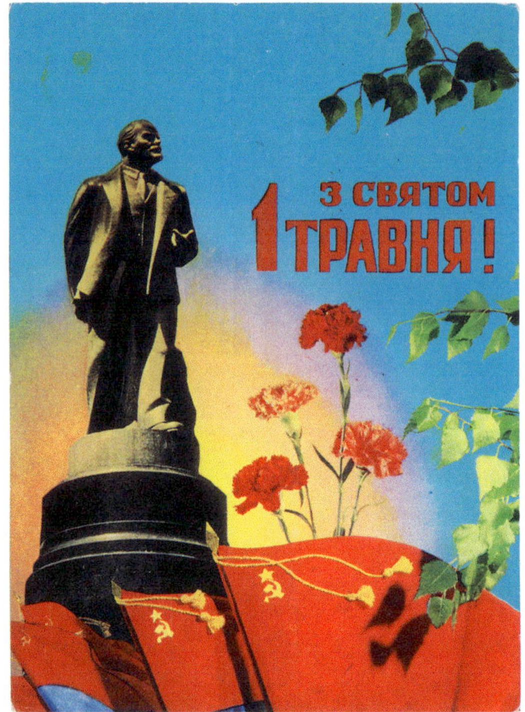

In the same way, we learned what 'Leninopad' meant in a Ukrainian context. This phenomenon was dictated not so much by historiographic logic as by civil and political imperatives, encouraged by strong nationalist movements. These elements were surrounded by a hefty administrative apparatus, which often made dialogue with local authorities difficult, if not absurd. In addition, decommunisation was taking place in the context of a dysfunctional, diversified state that was both poverty-stricken and at war. Decisions were not applied in the same way from one municipality to the next: everyone had their own interpretation. Here, there might be a 'civilised' decommunisation; there, a 'radical' demolition of Lenin. In one small village, a factory director pledged to defend the Lenin standing at the works entrance with his gun, shooting if necessary. In a neighbouring district, the mayor claimed there were insufficient funds in the municipal budget to dismantle the local Lenin. Original initiatives also appeared sporadically: Lenin was variously transformed into Darth Vader, a Cossack, or an Olympic champion.

Engulfing all these layers were the unavoidable components of contemporary Ukraine: abuse of power and corruption. The Kharkiv Lenin, the biggest in Ukraine when it fell, was made from pure bronze. The long days we spent in the city, going back and forth between administrators, journalists, civil militants and nationalists, led us to one simple conclusion: it had been stolen, melted down and sold. And nobody in Kharkiv seemed particularly bothered.

As our search continued, so the disappearance of the Bessarabska

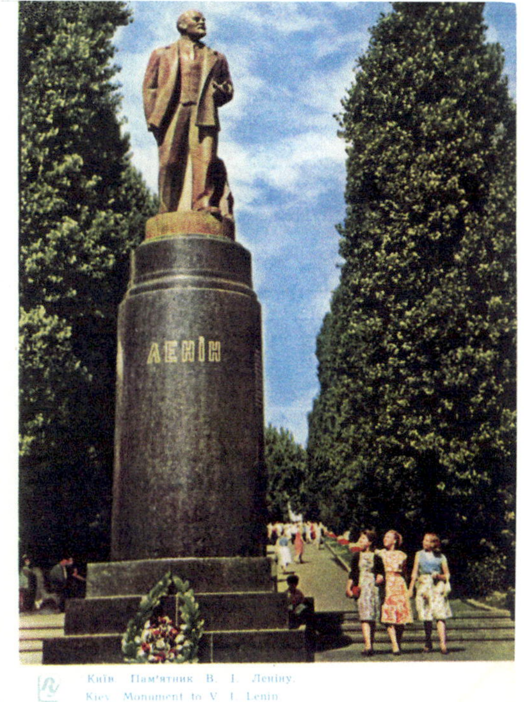

Kiev. Monument to V. I. Lenin.
Postcard, 1963

Lenin took on a symbolic dimension. It was no longer required for our project: we were already over-whelmed with all kinds of Lenins. But it mattered to us, as if it were a point of principle. It was an icon but also public property, and we had to gain access to it. And yet our belief in a positive outcome was waning.

LOSING OUR HEAD

'We must wait a little longer. We'll come back to it when the time is right.' This email from Vyacheslav in late January confirmed our suspicions. The Bessarabska Lenin would be very hard to find. Then came a long series of email exchanges containing photo-montages, full of promises and insinuations, all of which were completely absurd. One declared that Lenin's body had been given to the Kyiv municipal history museum. Except that no one at the museum had heard of it. Going from one false lead to the next, we started to imagine that Vyacheslav was enjoying giving us the run around. He had received the book we ordered from France, but it seemed unrealistic to expect anything from him in return – apart from ever increasing complications.

Of course, we persevered. Directly, but also through circles of acquaintances who were, to varying degrees, connected to the chief collector. Then, suddenly, an antiques dealer dropped us a line: 'The head is in Dnipro.' New lead, new hope. The head is not the body, of course, but maybe it would provide a resolution to our quest, especially since it took us back to our first lead: Eduard Leonov, the singer and former Svoboda parliamentarian, the patriot

167

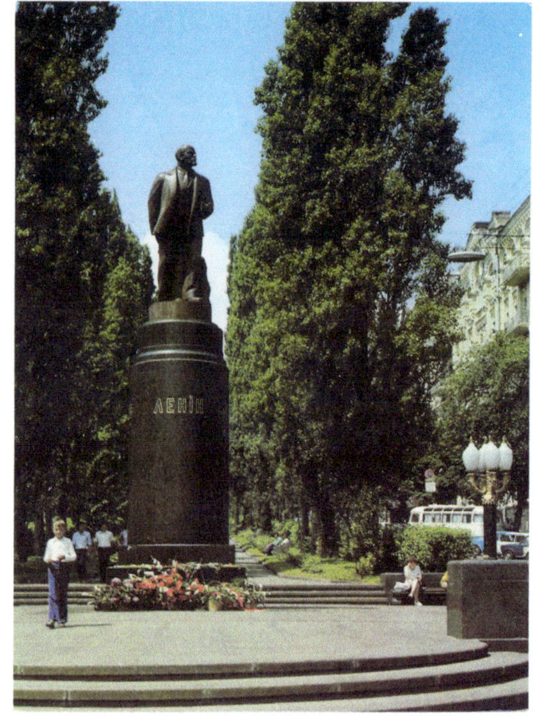

Kiev. Monument to V. I. Lenin.
Sculptor S. Merkurov
Architects A. Vlasov, V. Yelizarov
Postcard, 1979

with the Cossack haircut. This time we made contact. A smooth talker, he was one of the people who pulled Lenin to the ground on 8 December 2013. His hatred for this figure prevented him from keeping even a fragment. The head? He had no idea.

The only information he had to give us concerned 'a bit of hand that I gave to the history museum in Uzhhorod'. That was 800 kilometres from Kyiv, on the other side of the Carpathian Mountains, at the border with Slovakia. Yet another lovely journey through Western Ukraine, where Lenin was dethroned over twenty years ago. It is a fine autumn day and a beautiful route. The peaks of the Carpathians are already snow-capped. We have been hunting for the Bessarabska Lenin for over a year now. Finally, we are about to see the hand.

'The hand? We have a piece of beard in the museum.' Tomasz, a young activist in the local Svoboda branch, shows us the way. 'There, that's what we donated to the museum collection,' he says, pointing to a little pink pebble. Ah. A bit of the beard, or the hand, or the coat – it could be absolutely anything. But that doesn't even matter now. The simple fact that it is here, so far from Bessarabska Square, is a story in itself. We have found the Lenin that inspired us to find other Lenins. Even if the result is disappointing in reality, it doesn't detract from the sense of accomplishment. In this museum in Uzhhorod, our quest has ended.

A few days later, in Kyiv, we actually manage to find the head. The feeling is already less exhilarating. This is another piece of red quartzite, disfigured by hammer blows, that a Ukrainian deputy

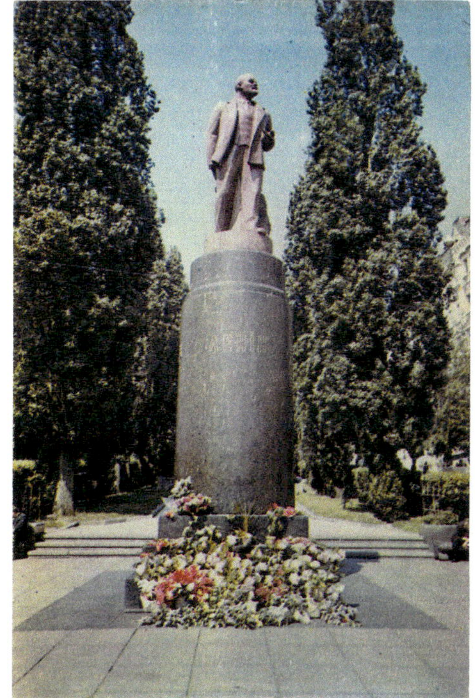

thought would look original mounted on metal spider's legs. Nothing news-worthy here.

QUESTIONS WITHOUT ANSWERS

The body? It's not essential any more. Maybe Vyacheslav and his chief collector are telling the truth? Maybe they no longer hold the statue? Maybe it's all bare-faced lies? Either way, their motives seem clear. Even if they are hiding behind the excuse of protecting their historical heritage, this debris of a monument has been stolen. The new owners took it from the community for their own exclusive use. In similar circumstances, other collectors would not hesitate to show their treasures, which only makes Vyacheslav's photomontages and false leads all the more disconcerting. Perhaps there's nothing to understand, or perhaps it is us who haven't completely understood?

It's just as well. The aim of this investigation was not to enable us to understand everything. It was never our ambition to come up with exhaustive answers to the questions raised by Ukrainian decommunisation. The point was to discover, to observe and to listen. And the result was a broad vision, a panorama, of an extremely complex process. The shadowy aspect of decommunisation and, in particular, the mystery surrounding the Bessarabska Lenin, are part of the tormented history of a country going through a profound transformation. What meaning will Ukrainians give their history? What will its impact be on current changes? And how can decommunisation influence ideas of national identity?

There is a lot to watch out for in this country. The fall of Lenin is only the beginning.

The smashed head of the Bessarabska Lenin (which stood on Bessarabska Square until December 2013) has been incorporated into this sculpture by Yuri Didovets. A lawyer, army officer and member of the city council, he makes furniture from used mortars, bomb-shell casings and other weapon parts as a hobby. The head stands in the corner of a room in his flat.
Kyiv. 4 November 2016

Over page left:
The left hand of the Bessarabska Lenin is now kept by Ihor Miroshnichenko, a Kyiv city council representative for the nationalist Svoboda ('Freedom') Party.
Kyiv. 16 February 2017

Over page right:
A piece of the Bessarabska Lenin (supposedly the elbow) is exhibited in the local history museum alongside objects from the Euromaidan revolution.
Museum of Regional History, Uzhhorod Castle, Uzhhorod. 2 November 2016

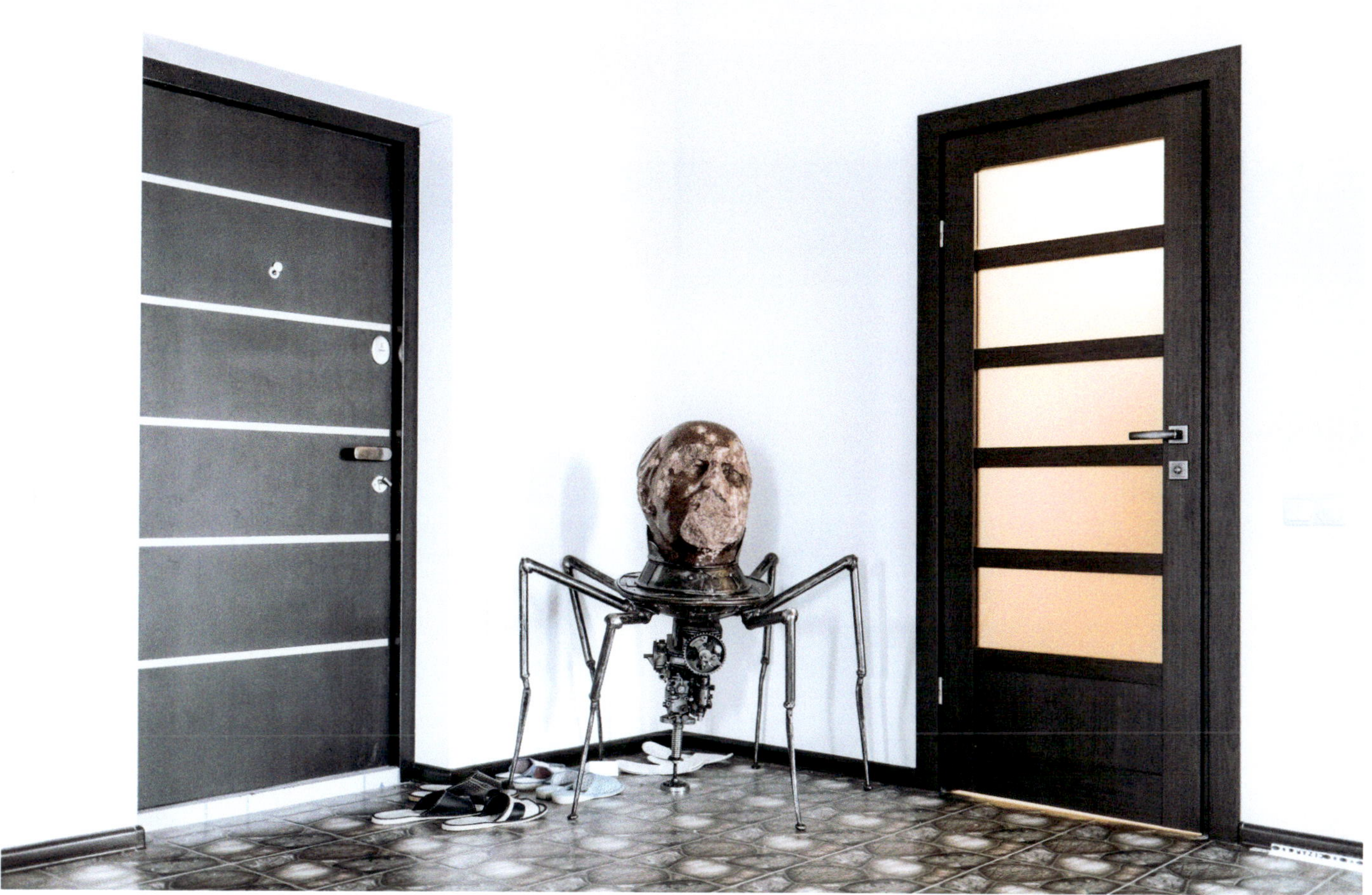

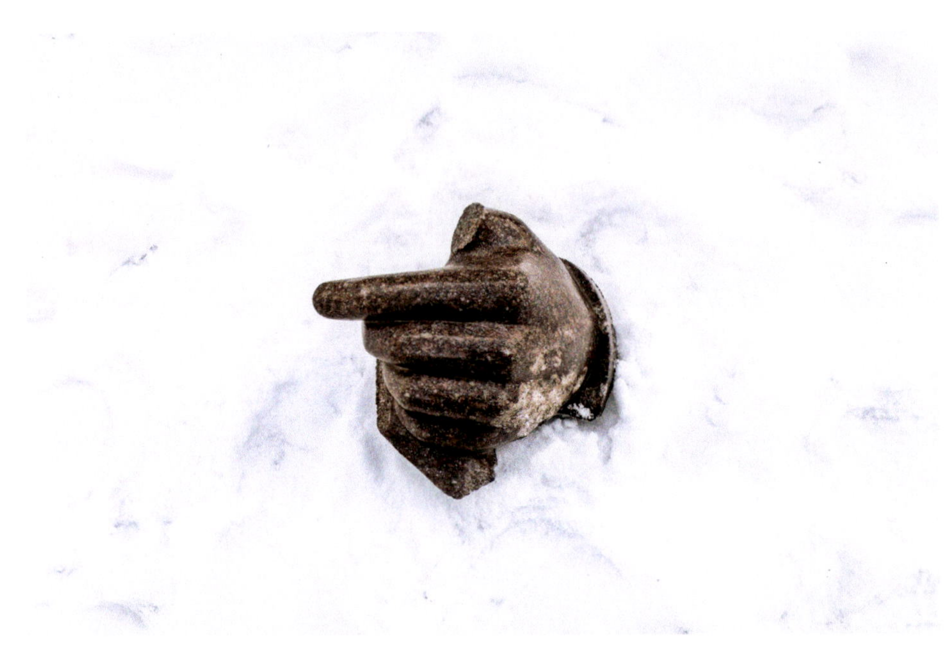

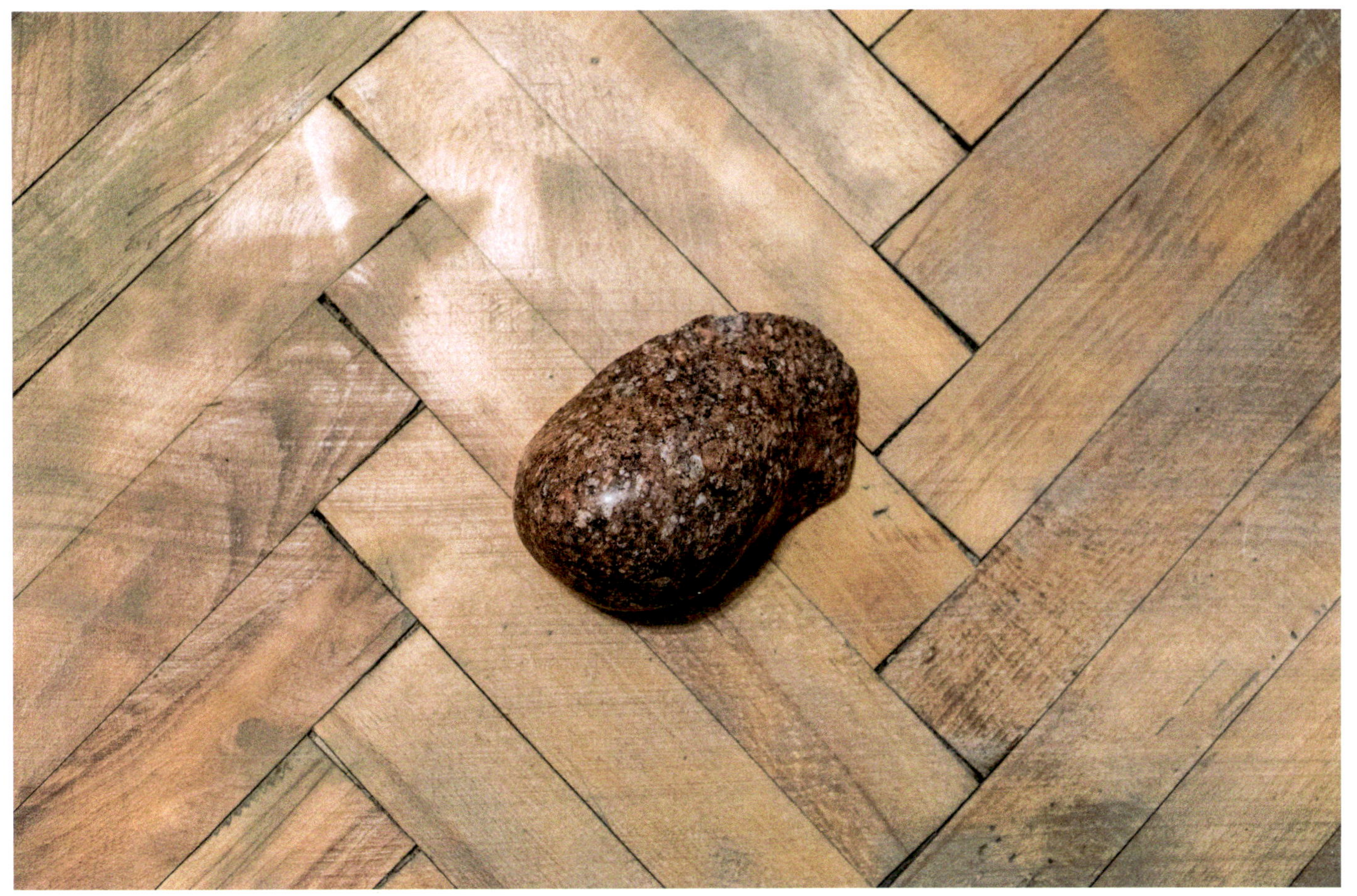

BIOGRAPHIES

Niels Ackermann (born 1987, Switzerland)
Ackermann is a Swiss photojournalist and founding member of the photography agency Lundi13. He has worked for the Swiss and international press since 2007. For his project *The White Angel* (Les Editions Noir Sur Blanc, 2016) he spent four years documenting the transition to adulthood of a group of youths near Chernobyl. He has received many awards, including the Prix de la Ville de Perpignan Rémi Ochlik 2016 and Swiss Press Photographer of the Year 2016. Ackermann uses documentary photography to reveal a more nuanced vision of Ukraine, that challenges stereotypes and gives a voice to contradictory opinions. He has exhibited in solo and group shows and festivals in Arles, Perpignan, Breda, Pingyao, Moscow, Kyiv, Zurich, Basel and Geneva. He has lived in Kyiv, Ukraine, since 2015.

Sébastien Gobert (born 1985, France)
After travelling extensively, Gobert became fascinated by post-Communist regions, living in many different countries across the area. In 2011 he settled in Ukraine, where he worked as a journalist, granting him a privileged perspective from which to observe the country's upheavals. He is a correspondent for *Libération*, Radio France Internationale, *Le Monde Diplomatique* and *La Tribune de Genève*, among others. He was awarded the 'Writing for CEE' award in 2013. In addition Gobert runs the blog *Nouvelles de l'Est* and is a contributing author to *Odyssée Européenne Dans L'Oeil des Géographes*, series of books addressing the subjective geography of European cities.

Myroslava Hartmond (born 1990, Ukraine)
Hartmond is a Research Associate at the Centre for International Studies, University of Oxford. She is the owner of Triptych: Global Arts Workshop, Ukraine.

Niels and Sébastien would like to thank the following people for their help with this project:

Béatrice and Marco Ackermann, Daphné Anglès, Manuel Bauer, Yulia Biletskaya, July Body, Lars Boering, Anna Bondar, Yurko Dosiak, James Erstin, Kateryna Filiuk, Michael Von Graffenried, The French Guy, Les Hawrylyshyn, Les Rencontres d'Arles, Vera Michalski Hoffmann, Gaël Hurlimann, Uliana Kabutta, Leonid Kanter, Tetiana Kozak, Eduard Leonov, Jean-Francois Leroy, Patrick Gilliéron LoHello, Romain Mader, Iuliia Mendel, Fred Merz, Yevgenia Moliar, Fanny Mossière, Damon Murray, Guillaume Perret, Peter Pfrunder, Liza Premiyak, Stéphane Rémael, Sasha Renner, Nicolas Righetti, Oleksiy Sheremetev, Patricia Shmorhun-Hawrylyshyn, Anna Shumeiko, Olga Shumeiko, Halyna Shyyan, Olga Sorin, Stephen Sorrell, Sam Stourdzé, Vladimir Subotovski, Olga Sviblova, Gaia Tripoli, Volodymyr Vyatrovych, François Wavre, Donald Weber, Patrick Witty, Igor Zinatulin.

Original cover image by Paul Cartron, from the project *Stakan*.

All postcards: FUEL archive

Painting on p.10: *Little Octobrists at the Monument to Vladimir Lenin* by Anatoly Plamenitsky, 1976. Courtesy: Myroslava Hartmond (Halushka) and Triptych: Global Arts Workshop.

Published in 2017

FUEL Design & Publishing
33 Fournier Street
London E1 6QE

fuel-design.com

Photographs © Niels Ackermann / Lundi13
Testimony texts © Sébastien Gobert
The Lenin Trail © Sébastien Gobert
Lenin After the Fall © Myroslava Hartmond

Design and edit by Murray & Sorrell FUEL

Distribution by Thames & Hudson / D. A. P.
ISBN: 978-0-9931911-7-6
Printed in Italy